12/07

CONTENTS :
1 v.
CD-ROM (1)

WITHDRAWN

Sourcebook of Scandinavian Furniture

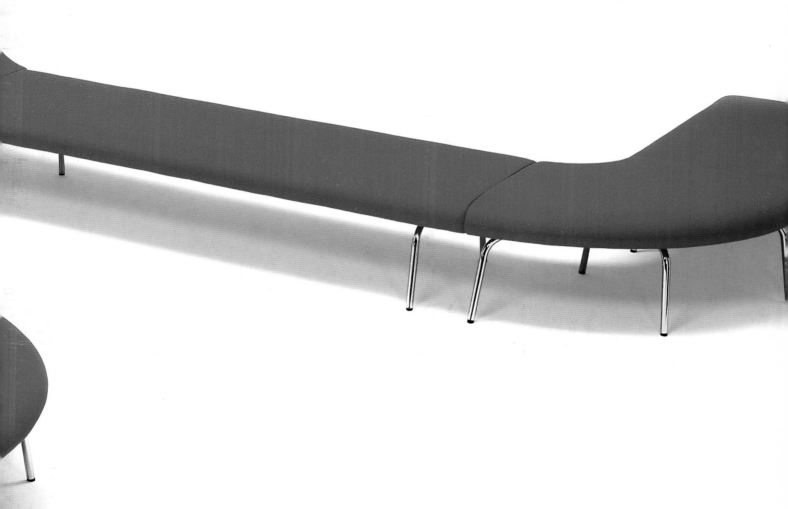

Sourcebook of Scandinavian Furniture

DESIGNS FOR THE 21st CENTURY

Judith Gura

W. W. NORTON & COMPANY | NEW YORK · LONDON

page 1: Parts of a Rainbow, Christian Flindt, 2004 (see also pages 56 and 139)
pages 2–3: Orbit Modular Seating, Eero Koivisto, 2001 (see also page 160)

For information about permission to reproduce selections from this book, write to
Permissions, W. W. Norton & Company, Inc., 500 Fifth Avenue, New York, NY 10110

Manufacturing by Colorprint
Book design by Kristina Kachele Design, llc
Production manager: Leeann Graham

Library of Congress Cataloging-in-Publication Data

Gura, Judith.
Sourcebook of Scandinavian furniture : designs for the 21st century / Judith Gura.
    p. cm.
Includes bibliographical references and index.
ISBN-13: 978-0-393-73151-4 (hardcover)
ISBN-10: 0-393-73151-0 (hardcover)
 1. Furniture design—Scandinavia—History—20th century.
 2. Furniture design—Scandinavia—History—21st century. I. Title.

NK2579.G87 2007
749.2809'04—dc22

                    2006100158

ISBN 13: 978-0-393-73151-4
ISBN 10: 0-393-73151-0

W. W. Norton & Company, Inc., 500 Fifth Avenue, New York, N.Y. 10110
www.wwnorton.com

W. W. Norton & Company Ltd., Castle House, 75/76 Wells Street, London W1T 3QT

0 9 8 7 6 5 4 3 2 1

To Meryl and Jeremy, who cut their teeth on Scandinavian furniture

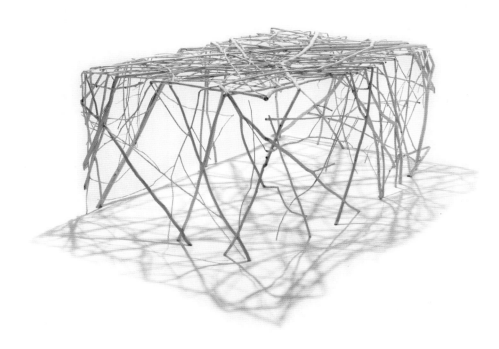

See page 61

See page 197

Contents

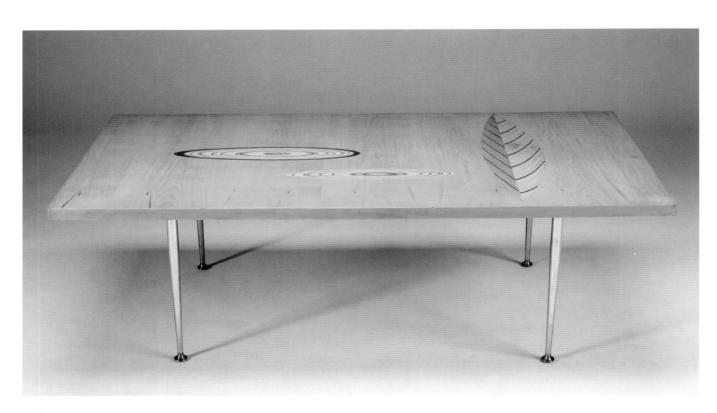

See page 39

Preface

This project began with the publisher's request for a sourcebook of Scandinavian furniture. The result is both somewhat less and something more. It is, in fact, a sampler showing only a small proportion of the extraordinary output of five countries, dozens of talented designers, and hundreds of producers. Along with the products, however, are several sections with historic details that tell the fascinating story of design in these countries.

The last serious American study of Scandinavian design, including furniture along with other categories, was published in 1982, a quarter-century ago, in conjunction with a major exhibition at the Cooper-Hewitt Museum (now the Cooper-Hewitt National Design Museum). Much has happened since then. To trace the origins of Scandinavian design, how it came into being, and how it has changed in recent years, I have included background information on each country, and have chronicled their combined developments in design and furniture production from the mid-twentieth century, when Scandinavian design became an international sensation, to the early years of the twenty-first century, as it has returned to prominence.

For readers familiar only with the earlier incarnation of Scandinavian design, the variety and range of today's products will come as a revelation. Of the several hundred objects illustrated in Section II on contemporary furniture, some were chosen for aesthetic appeal, some for inventive use of materials, some for technical achievements, and some for timelessness, but all for their excellence of design. Some were introduced more than seventy-five years ago, and others as recently as 2006. They were drawn from a variety of sources—large factories, modest workshops, and craft studios—some more than a century old and others newly founded. They constitute a limited sampling and a very personal one.

Chairs dominate the selection, as they do the entire output of the Nordic furniture industry, perhaps because they offer designers the greatest variety of individual expression. They can also be executed in the broadest possible range of materials and forms. Furnishings designed strictly for commercial use are not the focus of this book, though there are many items that can serve equally well in public or private spaces. Absent, too, are beds, which are most often made by specialty producers and conceived more as functional than fashionable pieces.

In exploring the "Scandinavian modern" phenomenon and its relation to contemporary furniture from Denmark, Finland, Iceland, Norway, and Sweden, it becomes clear how powerfully Nordic designers shaped our view of modernism. It also becomes clear how national design identity can be expressed—or obscured—in an increasingly multicultural world.

For readers familiar with design from the Nordic countries, and those about to become acquainted with it, I hope this book will provide insight and understanding of those nations' significant and continuing contributions to modern design.

Acknowledgments

As is always true of such detailed undertakings, many people contributed to the successful completion of this book. However, it could not have begun without Claes Jernaeus, whose invitation to examine contemporary design in Sweden opened my eyes to a new view of Nordic design, and sparked my desire to write about it. I thank him, Inger and Olle Wastberg, and their colleagues in New York and Stockholm. Their counterparts at the Consulates General of Finland, Norway, and Iceland encouraged and assisted my exploration of design in the Nordic countries, and The Danish Design Center, Svensk Form, Norsk Form, and Design Forum Finland supplied background information and introductions to designers and manufacturers during several research trips. Special thanks to Ilkka Kalliomaa, Eva Vincent, Svanhvit Adalsteinsdottir, Adalstein Ingolfsson, Birgitta Capetillo, Kirstin and Birgitta Bjerregaard, and others I have not named, but have not forgotten.

I am grateful to the producers and designers who accommodated my requests for images, to those e-mail correspondents who graciously answered my repeated inquiries, and to Paul Jackson, for invaluable access to his vast database of furniture images.

Thanks to my research assistants: Rita Jules for preliminary image searches, Monica Obniski for collecting and organizing images, photo files and publication clearances, and Jill Gustafson for collating details from disparate sources in several languages for the designer biographies.

For transforming a manuscript into a beautiful book, I thank Nancy Green, a patient and caring hands-on editor who steered the project through every challenging stage; Kristina Kachele, for a design as visually appealing as the objects it showcases; Johanna Zacharias, for copy-editing, Kristen Holt-Browning and Vani Kannan who juggled the details, and the supportive staff at W. W. Norton. And as always, I thank Martin for his impeccable critical sense, eagle-eye final reading, and unwavering support. The merits of this publication are largely the responsibility of these people. Its failings, omissions, or inaccuracies are mine.

See page 190

PART I

The Nordic Nations & Modern Design

How did five small countries not previously noted for aesthetic leadership create a style that dominated the international marketplace for almost a quarter of the last century? The phenomenon that was Scandinavian design cannot be attributed to any single factor. It was enabled by fortuitous social and political events, but its evolution can be traced in the individual but interrelated histories of the Nordic nations.

Although the groundswell of modern design that reached its apex in the United States and Western Europe in the mid-twentieth century is most often traced to the avant garde of Continental Europe, many of modernism's most productive seeds were sown in the cluster of countries to the north, whose similar traditions provided fertile soil for the growth of a common aesthetic. These countries had brilliant designers, innovative manufacturers and astute marketers, but so did other centers of design. The unique determinants of their extraordinary success were the character of the people and a cultural climate that nurtured their particular attitude toward design—one in which the integrity of each object was more important than the pursuit of fashion.

The story of Scandinavian design has been translated only in part and not altogether accurately. Though broadly accepted and used, the term itself is a construct, and ambiguous in meaning. Scandinavia in fact consists of just three countries—Denmark, Norway, and Sweden—the northwestern European nations that share both geographic affinity and related languages. Together with Finland and Iceland, they constitute the Nordic nations. To much of the world, however, Scandinavia connotes all five.

Despite its widespread use, the term "Scandinavian design," in designating objects from the Nordic nations in the mid-twentieth century, does not define a particular style. It is not about a single silhouette or shape of leg or ornament. Rather, it refers to an aesthetic approach that is shared by all five countries—an attitude toward design that reflects a particular view of the environment and the objects that furnish it. This attitude emerges directly from the countries' cultural backgrounds and their related histories, which are summarized in the following pages.

Even the strongest and most secure of the Scandinavian nations, Denmark and Sweden, looked to Continental European styles for inspiration until the late nineteenth century, finding their own design directions only in the twentieth century. To varying degrees, all have retained many folk customs, including strong crafts traditions that are reflected even in factory-produced goods. Of all the industrialized nations, the Nordic countries have been most successful in moving into the modern world without breaking with the past. Perhaps in part because they came relatively late to industrialization, they forged comfortable alliances between art and design, between machine production and handwork, usually managing to combine the best features of both. By the middle of the twentieth century, they were producing some of the world's most admired objects.

Viewing design as an integral part of everyday life, with strong links to national folk and crafts traditions, Nordic designers melded these concepts with the newly minted modernity of their Continental counterparts. In their interpretation of modern design, beauty and function were interdependent; objects were meant to be used, rather than merely admired. These designers were less concerned with newness for its own sake than they were with finding timeless solutions to specific needs. Produced by like-minded manufacturers, their designs were easy to understand, attractive, and for the most part affordable.

The Nordic version of accessible modernism was most often referred to as humanistic. It emphasized simplicity and natural materials, but more important, it implied a concern for the user in furniture that looked inviting, was pleasing to the touch, and was comfortable to use. In this, it provided an alternative to the hard-edged severity of many objects following the aesthetic of the Bauhaus, the German school considered to be the seminal source of twentieth-century modernism. The intellectual appeal of geometric forms of glass, leather, and steel were difficult for many consumers to understand. Not so the softer curves of Scandinavian modern. The Nordic countries became associated with good modern design—not always the most innovative, or even the most celebrated, but certainly the most consistent.

In the 1950s, the mystique of "Scandinavian design" was embraced by an international clientele, aided by inventive promotion and marketing efforts that positioned it prominently in much of the western world for more than two decades. These included major presentations at the important Triennale di Milano trade fair—which yielded literally dozens of international awards for designers in Finland, Denmark, Sweden, and Norway. In addition, image-building exhibitions of Scandinavian objects, often cooperative efforts among the countries, sparked a surge of interest and, more important, an explosion of exports.

The influence of Scandinavian modernism has been extraordinary, particularly in view of the relatively modest size and economic position of the countries from which it was generated. As *New York Times* reporter Rita Reif wrote in 1982, "Scandinavian Design *was* modern for a generation of Americans." As a result, worldwide recognition accrued to many of its designers. It was also an important influence on interpretations of modern design in other countries, most particularly the United States and Great Britain, whose contemporary furniture designs clearly owe much to Nordic style. The understated lines, natural materials, and emphasis on quality and timelessness rather than on trend-setting style contributed both to the success of Scandinavian design and to its eventual fall from grace. The same characteristics that made it most appealing also made it predictable—a fatal handicap in a marketplace driven by fashion change.

In recent years, the cycles of revivalism have returned Scandinavian modern furniture to center stage. While some mid-century modernism is a fashion already fading, however, the qualities that distinguished mid-century Scandinavian design continue to inform objects created in the new materials and advanced technologies by today's second and third generations of Nordic designers. As is the case with all of their contemporaries, today's designers are inclined to speak, aesthetically, in similar tongues. In subtle ways, nevertheless, they are still carrying on a tradition begun more than a century ago by the Swedish critic who proclaimed the need for "more beautiful things for everyday use."

DENMARK

At 43,000 square kilometers (less than 17,000 square miles), the Kingdom of Denmark is the smallest of the Nordic nations. Its population of 5.5 million inhabits a peninsula joined at the south end to the European continent and more than 400 islands linked by a network of bridges. Both Greenland and the Faeroe Islands are self-governing parts of Denmark. A farming country with little in the way of natural resources, Denmark has always depended on importing essential goods. These, in turn, are supported by exports, of which furniture and agriculture are the most important components. A strong merchant fleet helps the Danes to maintain a balanced economy and a high standard of living.

A constitutional monarchy since 1849, Denmark was an independent and powerful nation by the eleventh century, when it controlled most of what is now Scandinavia as well as part of England. Denmark was the dominant member of the Kalmar Union, in which it joined with Sweden and Norway in 1397 as a means of checking the increasing power of the Germany-based Hanseatic League. This alliance of three independent kingdoms under a single monarch, which lasted until 1523, is largely responsible for the common Nordic culture that exists today. Despite a strong sense of national identity, and a craft tradition dating to the eleventh century when the Vikings ruled Denmark (as well as Norway, England, and part of Sweden), the country's primary design influences came from its closest Continental neighbors—Germany (with which it shares a border), England, and France.

Of all the Nordic nations, Denmark has the strongest heritage of furniture making—one that dates back several centuries. The Royal Academy of Fine Arts, founded in 1754, included craft as well as fine arts in its curriculum, and the state-supported Royal Furniture Emporium, operating from 1777 to 1815, provided an outlet for handcrafted goods and established criteria for quality workmanship. Thus began a tradition of superlative craftsmanship that endures to the present. Special craft schools began in the nineteenth century, and Danish applied arts were shown in 1857 at the Great Exhibition in London as well as the Paris Exposition Universelle of 1900. The Danish Society for Arts and Crafts was established in 1907, and remains active today.

Though quality of craft was an ongoing concern, attention to originality of design came later. Until the beginning of World War I, Danish furniture reflected European styles, from Baroque to Rococo to Neoclassical to a variant of Jugendstil called *Skonvirke* (works of beauty). The first signs of change came in 1914 at the Nordic Exhibition in Malmö, where designs in the handicraft tradition contrasted with those moving towards functionalism. Copenhagen, which had by then become the art center of Scandinavia, later produced a version of French *art moderne*, though it was not widely accepted by Danish traditionalists, who looked to classical forms for inspiration. Many of the exhibits in Kaj Fisker's striking pavilion at the 1925 Paris Exposition Internationale des Arts Décoratifs et Industriels Modernes were neoclassical, though designer and critic Poul Henningsen's publication, *Kritisk Revy* (Critical Review), took on the establishment in his call for a new approach to social consciousness and originality in design.

The roots of modern Danish furniture are generally traced to the establishment, in 1924, of a Department of Furniture and Interior Decoration

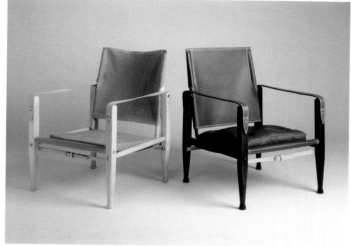

I-00I
Faaborg Chair, Kaare Klint, 1914
Cabinetmaker: Rud. Rasmussen
Producer: Rud. Rasmussen
(see also page 84)

I-002
Safari Chairs, Kaare Klint, 1930
Cabinetmaker: Rud. Rasmussen
Producer: Rud. Rasmussen
www.Jacksons.se
(see also page 84)

I-003
Palisander Cabinet, Ole Wanscher, 1940s
Cabinetmaker: A. J. Iverson
Not in current production
Collection: Vance Trimble

at Copenhagen's Academy of Fine Arts, soon under the direction of architect and designer Kaare Klint. Although Klint's own approach was historicist, and his aesthetic reflected eighteenth-century styles (mostly English), Klint influenced two generations of furniture designers. Of particular import were his innovative studies in what would later be called ergonomics, in which he developed a system of measurements based on human proportions to be used in determining the dimensions of furniture. Another influential designer, Ole Wanscher, studied historic furniture in research that was put to practical use by a next generation of designers.

In the years after World War I (the 1920s and 1930s), new housing with smaller rooms created a demand for simple, well-proportioned furniture, and Danish designers began to concern themselves with unpretentious everyday objects. The Danish Export Council encouraged the production of moderate-priced furniture for possible export and, during World War II, a collection of practical designs by Borge Mogensen was produced by the Danish Cooperative Wholesale Society and shown at the 1944 Malmö Housing Exhibition. The Danes, along with the Swedes, worked out the concept of what was referred to as K-D (knock-down) furniture, which could be sold disassembled and put together by the consumer—a concept that facilitated shipping, reduced costs, and therefore encouraged exports.

Danish furniture makers tended to focus more on the process of craft than on defining a particular aesthetic. This began to change after the Cabinetmakers Guild, an association of small workshops, decided to schedule annual exhibitions as a means of promoting business during the Depression. The exhibitions, held at Copenhagen's Kunstindustrimuseum (Museum of Decorative Arts) from 1927 through 1966 celebrated craftsmanship at a time when those skills were declining elsewhere. Beginning in 1939, design competitions were held before each show, stimulating innovation and ultimately producing the iconic designs celebrated as "Danish Modern" furniture. The cabinetmakers crafted finished

1-004

1-004
Spoke-back Sofa, Borge Mogensen, 1945
Producer: Fredericia
(see also page 172)

models of the winning entries, in return for which the designers arranged the displays. Most pieces were marked with the names of both designer and craftsman, giving equal importance to both, and forging partnerships whose furniture put Denmark in the forefront of Scandinavian modernism. Without pressure to produce in quantity, there was no need to cut corners on workmanship, and the exhibitions became showplaces for superlative craftsmanship and design. Designers used the shows as opportunities to find producers for their work, and manufacturers used them as sources of new ideas; when pieces were adapted for production, Denmark's modest-size producers adapted studio techniques to manufacturing facilities to produce pieces as well made as the prototypes. The alliances that developed from these collaborations between designers and producers were unique to Denmark.

The refined classical shapes of Hans Wegner, the organic forms of Finn Juhl, the practical designs of Mogens Koch, and works by other celebrated designers such as Mogens Lassen, Peter Hvidt, Grete Jalk, and Borge Mogensen were introduced at the Cabinetmakers Guild exhibitions. Most of these first-generation Danish furniture designers were themselves trained cabinetmakers and hence were able to transform their ideas into objects that could actually be made. Their approach to modern design emphasized natural materials and simple forms, without pretension and generally without ornament. Unlike their colleagues in neighboring Nordic countries who used blond native woods, however, the Danish cabinetmakers most often turned to imported teak from Thailand and rosewood from Brazil. The rich patina and decorative grains of these woods, though without the glossy polish of traditional wood furniture (most Danish furniture was maintained simply by rubbing with boiled

1-005

1-006

1-005
Pelikan Chair, Finn Juhl, 1940
Cabinetmaker: Niels Vodder
Producer: Hansen & Sorensen
(reintroduced 2005)
(see also page 119)

1-006
China Chair, Hans Wegner, 1944
Cabinetmaker: Johannes Hansen
Current Producer: PP Møbler
(another version by Fritz Hansen)
(see also page 72)

linseed oil), gave the furniture an elegant look that positioned it at the higher end of the market. The rich look was retained even in production versions of the designs in rosewood, teak, and often also in walnut, a wood that was more familiar to consumers.

Despite occasional echoes of classical form, the Danish designs owed nothing to the folk tradition or ethnic inspirations seen in Norwegian, Icelandic, and some Finnish designs. Taking national identity for granted, the Danes had no need to express it in design. The understated sophistication of Danish furniture of this era broadened its appeal, and was a contributing factor in its exceptional international success.

Though occupied by Germany during World War II, Denmark, unlike Norway, suffered no physical damage and was able to return rapidly to normal, pre-war furniture production. In the postwar decades, thanks in large part to astute marketing and promotion on the part of both governmental and commercial groups, Danish furniture spearheaded the international acceptance of Scandinavian design. The phrase "Danish modern" supplanted "Swedish modern" as the mantra of sophisticated consumers, feeding the demand for an accessible genre of contemporary furniture to fit the restricted spaces of new houses and apartments. Danish furniture was shown, and honored, at the prestigious Triennale fairs in Milan, and Denmark participated in international events and promotions along with its Nordic neighbors, where Danish furniture became the paradigm of Scandinavian modern. The retail store Den Permanente opened in downtown Copenhagen in 1931 as an association of crafts studios supported by the Danish Society of Arts and Crafts. It became a tourist attraction, promotional vehicle, and product showcase, making international stars of Kaj Boisen (wood toys), Björn Winblad (whimsical ceramics), and Ib

1-007

1-008

1-009

Antoni (posters), while the prestige of Royal Copenhagen porcelain and Georg Jensen silver (a Georg Jensen store had been in New York since 1924) spilled over to benefit all aspects of Danish design. Widely admired and emulated, Danish color schemes of soft neutrals and earth tones were a calm complement to the bold hues of modern art.

Flush with success, the Danes resisted the temptation to change styles simply for the sake of fashion. But as they continued to design what the market had embraced, innovation was gradually replaced by predictability and uninspired look-alikes. The industrialization of the furniture business in the late 1960s ended the cabinetmaker–designer collaborations, and many of the cabinetmakers' businesses closed; of the most celebrated, only Rud. Rasmussen is still operating. Den Permanente closed in 1988, ending another stimulus to creative design. Despite the continuing high quality of Danish furniture, what was perceived as a sameness of style (and rising prices) in a fashion-conscious market ultimately led to its decline, and Danish design lost its cutting edge.

In recent years, however, a new generation of young designers has begun to move out of the shadows of their lionized predecessors. Trained

1-007
Highback Chair, Fritz Henningsen, 1947
Not in current production
www.Jacksons.se

1-008
Revolving Bookcase, Mogens Koch, 1938
Cabinetmaker: Rud. Rasmussen
Producer: Rud. Rasmussen

1-009
Z-Down Chair, Erik Magnussen, 1940
Producer: Engelbrechts
(see also page 123)

at the architecture and design schools in Copenhagen and Århus, and international in their approach, they have brought new vigor and creativity to Danish furniture, which has begun to recapture its prestige in the international marketplace.

FINLAND

Along with Iceland, the northernmost of the Nordic countries, Finland—*Suomi* in its own tongue—is separated from the others by three factors. Its climate is the least forgiving, since one-third of Finland's 337,000-square-kilometer land mass (some 130,000 square miles) lies within the Arctic Circle. Its topography—three-fourths covered by forest—includes 60,000 lakes, more than any other country in the world. And its language is unrelated to that of any of its neighbors, bearing common elements only with Estonian, Hungarian, and some Russian. (Bringing them closer to their Nordic neighbors, however, Finland's 5.2 million citizens are bilingual—Finnish and Swedish are both official languages).

Though settled in prehistoric times, Finland did not come easily to an independent identity. It was dominated for centuries by larger and more powerful neighbors. Ruled by Sweden from the twelfth century, it was ceded to Russia in 1809 after the Napoleonic wars. Despite its relative autonomy as a grand duchy, Finland sought more, and in the wake of the Russian Revolution, declared itself an independent republic in 1917.

In a period measured in decades rather than centuries, Finland made the transition from a rural economy to a highly industrialized nation. Since most of its existing structures were built after independence, it is a land of modern architecture, and its citizens have a consuming interest in design, which is debated in the press with the intensity of political issues.

In their search for a national character, the Finns, more than any other Nordic nation, have used design as a means of self-definition. While reflecting ties to the Arts and Crafts movement, to Art Nouveau, and to Jugendstil, Finnish styles drew their strongest inspiration from indigenous tradition. The distinctive style called National Romanticism, emerging in the late nineteenth century, focused on Finland's unique heritage. The most important inspiration came from the *Kalevala*, a series of allegorical epic poems of mythological Finnish heroes retold as oral history from generation to generation in the language of Karelia, Finland's much-disputed far northeastern province. Transcribed in Finnish (a language not previously used for written works) and published only in 1835, the *Kalevala* provided folklore and imagery that became touchstones for nationalistic fervor, inspiring artistic expression in many areas (including Jean Sibelius's stirring "Finlandia" orchestral suite). It was National Romanticism, rather than expressions of modern design, that first brought Finland to international attention, in the pavilion designed by Eliel Saarinen and his associates Herman Geselius and Armas Lindgren,

1-010
Paimio Chair, Alvar Aalto, 1931
Original Producer: Huonekalu-ja-
Rakennustyötehdas
Current Producer: Artek
www.Jacksons.se

1-010

at the 1900 Exposition Universelle in Paris. Building on this success, the
Finnish Fair Corporation, since 1920, has implemented exhibition show-
ings to highlight Finnish design.

In the last quarter of the nineteenth century, the Finns established several institutions to nurture design: The Museum of Art and Design (1873),
the oldest existing Nordic museum of its kind, the Finnish Society of
Crafts and Design (1875), to promote Finnish skill in applied art, and the
Friends of Finnish Handicrafts (1894), which staged competitions that
also stimulated furniture design.

In the 1930s, the Functionalist movement (called *Funkis* in Finland)
called for a rejection of historicism, following the dictates of European
modernism. The Finns, however, departed from the more severe Swedish
version of the style, adapting to industrialized production with spare,
simple forms that retained links to Finland's rural heritage. Lacking natural resources such as gold, stones, and rare woods to make luxury products, Finnish designers focused on everyday goods—a practical decision
that helped them cope with the dual challenges of economic depression
and postwar shortages.

The story of Finnish modern furniture from 1930 to 1950 can be told
in two words: Alvar Aalto. The leading Finnish architect and designer
of the twentieth century, Aalto is recognized as one of the world's most

1-011

important as well. His cantilever chairs of laminated plywood (based on nineteenth-century technology developed by Thonet in Germany) laid the groundwork for designs by Marcel Breuer, Charles Eames, and other celebrated modernists. In 1935 he founded Artek to market his furniture internationally (a New York retail shop opened in 1940). After the war he taught at the Massachusetts Institute of Technology. (Since 1926, Finnish emigré Eliel Saarinen, president of Cranbrook Academy, in Bloomfield Hills, Michigan, had been training young American designers-to-be including Charles Eames and his own son, Eero.)

In the catalog preface for a 1938 exhibition of Aalto's work at the Museum of Modern Art in New York City, curator John McAndrew referred to Finnish design as "unencumbered by reverence for past styles and conventions." Finland's growing recognition in the international marketplace was assured with Aalto's acclaimed national exhibit at the 1939 New York World's Fair, a striking environment evoking Finnish forests and lakes.

Having come relatively late to industrialization, the Finns developed production methods that combined craft and machine skills, making the most of available indigenous materials—birch, pine, and spruce. A furniture industry developed in southern Finland around the area of Lahti. Without established style traditions to follow, Finnish designers enjoyed considerable freedom of creative expression, and pioneers such as Arttu Brummer and Ilmari Tapiovaara contributed to the evolving spectrum of Finnish design, which was assiduously marketed at major fairs. Finland became a regular participant—and a consistent medal-winner—in such events, beginning in Monza, Italy, in 1925, and from 1933 on at the Triennale fairs in Milan, which became the most prominent international celebration of design. National competitions were held to solicit new designs suitable for the exhibitions, which encouraged such designers as Tapio Wirkkala and Timo Sarpaneva, and provided prominent showcases for their achievements. The fairs commanded worldwide attention, bringing considerable prestige to Finnish design in furniture, glass, ceramics, and the shaggy loop-pile riijy rugs, better known as *ryas*. Later, in the 1970s, the popularity of innovative Marimekko fabrics and clothing helped maintain Finland's design identity even as enthusiasm for Scandinavian style was waning.

By the years just preceding World War II, Finland had perfected the spare and simple aesthetic that distinguishes much of its modern design, and was poised to become a challenger in the international marketplace. When the war ended, accelerated urbanization brought a demand for new products for the domestic market, while economic deficits impelled the need to find export markets abroad. But there was a more pressing imperative: the requirement to pay war reparations to Russia. This was an unexpected stimulant to the development of the Finnish furniture industry. Finnish designers accepted the mandate to produce salable goods as a creative challenge, shifting their focus from utilitarian objects to designed ones, with the support of small manufacturers willing to try something new. The results were favorable, both aesthetically and economically.

From mid-century on, Finland was an enthusiastic and willing participant in joint promotional efforts with its neighbors—an astute and very successful move. Particularly in the postwar years, this link to the other Nordic nations helped to identify Finland as politically neutral, dissociating it from the Eastern bloc and avoiding the "downscale" image of the Baltic countries.

Along with a distinctive aesthetic that is perhaps more austere than those of Finland's Nordic neighbors, Finnish design resonates with its connection to the landscape of the country, its lakes and woodlands. The Finns (and the Norwegians) are still taught crafts in school, and their designs are often spare, functional forms drawn from nature, exploiting the natural pine and birch grain and tactile qualities of wood and avoiding superfluous decoration. The color palette is light and also nature-inspired.

Having successfully embraced modernism without entirely breaking with tradition, Finnish modern design is notable for its originality and its fondness for innovation and experiment. But its international success can be attributed to other factors as well: strong government sponsorship,

THE NORDIC NATIONS & MODERN DESIGN

supportive craft societies, and the shrewd use of international fairs as promotional vehicles. As historian Kaj Kalin comments, "Finland was rebuilt with the images of design: in Finland, design has been a national project."

ICELAND

Often described as a European island in the North Atlantic, Iceland is strikingly different from the other Nordic nations and in many ways is the least "Scandinavian." Situated some 1,000 kilometers (670 miles) west of Norway, its closest neighbor, Iceland is a la nd of dramatic topography. Glaciers cover 11 percent of its 100,000 square kilometers (nearly 40,000 square miles); mountains, volcanoes, and underground hot springs account for much of the rest. With ten thousand waterfalls, Iceland has more hydroelectric capacity than any other country in the world. A small and homogenous population of fewer than three hundred thousand speaks a language related to Old North German; the tongue has changed little since the thirteenth century.

The first inhabitants of Iceland, the last country in Europe to be settled, were Vikings and Celts, who arrived and took possession in the ninth and tenth centuries. Iceland remained independent for three centuries (establishing the *Althing*, the world's oldest functioning legislature, in the tenth century) before coming under rule first by Norway and then Denmark. Iceland was granted independence in 1918, though it remained under the aegis of the Danish king, and finally proclaimed itself a constitutional republic in 1944.

Held back by centuries of foreign rule, Iceland was also subject to physical misfortune. Plagues decimated the population in the eighteenth

I-012
Kitchen Settee, Sveinn Kjarval, 1951–52
Collection: Museum of Design/Applied
Art, Iceland

I-012

century, and heavy volcanic activity caused famines, leading to the emigration of almost 20 percent of its population in the late nineteenth century. When the twentieth century began, Iceland was perhaps Europe's most primitive country. Although it was a late starter in its move into the modern age, once development began Iceland's progress was swift. In the years since World War II it has evolved into a modern nation, with some industry and a sophisticated service economy. Its primary export is fish—a vital asset since, like Denmark, Iceland must import virtually all of its raw materials.

Despite a strong cultural heritage in literature and music, Iceland, for so many centuries an agrarian community, has little tradition in design. Its enduring folk culture (and a storied belief in elves—the magical *huldufólk*), however, contributed a vocabulary of images reflected in carving, needlework, and weaving. As early as 1900, the country's craft skills were gaining notice beyond its shores—Iceland exhibited furniture at the Paris Exposition Universelle, though with objects carved in medieval style rather than the then-fashionable Art Nouveau style.

Traditionally, Icelandic furniture had been home-crafted rather than designed and fabricated, and made in the simplest possible forms as basic fittings for the turf houses and huts in which most Icelanders lived until after the beginning of the century. It was generally of dark-toned local woods ornamented with carvings of folklore motifs. In the 1920s, Icelandic designers began to travel abroad to study—initially to Germany, and later to Denmark and Sweden—and these outside influences began to dominate Icelandic design, introducing the concepts of modernism. Traces of modern design are seen in the classically inspired public buildings designed by Gudjon Samuelsson, named the first National Architect of Iceland in 1919, whose spare interiors and furniture hint at a twentieth-century aesthetic. Functionalism was introduced into domestic interiors by Sigurdur Gudmundsson in the late 1920s, and a 1932 industrial exhibition in the capital city of Reykjavik showed the first identifiably modern furniture—including objects of tubular metal.

When the approach of World War II restricted study overseas, the School of Applied Art, established in Reykjavik in 1939, gave Icelandic designers the opportunity to break free of outside influence. Like the Finns, and the Norwegians as well, the Icelanders sought an expression of national style, and, like the others, found it in vernacular tradition and objects. Until very recently, arts education in Iceland focused

1-013

1-013
Armchair, Sveinn Kjarval, 1951–52
Collection: Museum of Design/Applied
Art, Iceland

primarily on crafts, and though the level of craftsmanship has been extremely high, design was not identified as a separate discipline. *Hönnun,* the Icelandic word for design, came into the language only in the mid-twentieth century.

By that time, Iceland had become known for its high-quality knitwear and furs, but a scarcity of raw materials—even the wood for furniture is imported—and the lack of production facilities limited the development of a furniture industry comparable to those in the other Nordic countries. Urbanization after World War I had encouraged the development of local furniture workshops, with trained craftsmen immigrating from Germany, and though a fledgling industry had begun to evolve in the following decades, most of those factories closed when the boom in Scandinavian furniture waned in the 1970s. Unable to compete with the diversity of products from the Continent in the era of the Common Market and broader international trade, Icelandic industry, with occasional exceptions, is mostly devoted to products related to commercial fishing.

Iceland's greatest handicap in the development of design, however, has been its centuries of physical and cultural isolation. Iceland did not participate in most of the joint Nordic promotion activities (though it was part of the Danish exhibit at the 1939 New York World's Fair), owing not only to its isolation but also to the absence of governmental and organizational support such as those in the other countries. On the other hand, Icelanders' sense of separation has had a positive effect on the Icelandic character, being largely responsible for an admirable independence of spirit. What Icelandic designers have most in common seems to be their individuality. Another defining characteristic is their fierce attachment to their homeland—even those who studied abroad have tended to return home to practice, and most have been more interested in producing objects for their own countrymen than in designing for foreign markets.

Working under conditions that would prove daunting to less hardy spirits, Iceland's resourceful young designers today are seeking—and finding—various outlets for their talents, turning out increasingly sophisticated designs that are bringing new attention to their originality. Unimpeded by a traditional identity to maintain, they find unexpected solutions to the problems of marrying crafts and design. They treat the high cost of importing materials, the scarcity of local production facilities, and the difficulties of exporting as challenges rather than handicaps. Some have established their own studios for craft-centered production; others have found manufacturers abroad to produce their furniture. Many work in several disciplines, finding opportunities in more than one specialty—designing glass and textiles, interior design or architecture as well as furniture. Taking advantage of their accessibility to both Europe and North America, they are broadening their scope and learning to market themselves beyond their national borders: in a program initiated in 1999 at the forward-thinking Iceland Academy of the Arts, for example, marketing and business skills are taught along with design. And technology has benefited them as well—with no need for imported raw materials, Icelandic graphic design has gained renown for cutting-edge creativity.

In the past several years, the government has taken a more supportive attitude toward all areas of design, recognizing its value to the country's identity as progressive and culturally sophisticated. The founding of a Museum of Design and Applied Art in 1998 reflects a growing awareness of the importance of this area. With a more sympathetic government, more advanced educational programs, and increasing participation with its neighbors in promotional activities, Icelandic design in furniture as well as craft-related objects is finally seeking its place in the international market, and may, in the long run, provide the secret ingredient in a new recipe for Scandinavian design.

NORWAY

Norway, the western part of the Scandinavian peninsula, with about the same area as Finland, has an Ice Age landscape of fjords, forests, and mountains. Norway has more coastline in proportion to its area than any other urban country in the world. Not surprisingly, it is a maritime nation, with seafaring skills that date back to the legendary Vikings, as well as major shipbuilding and fishing industries. At 4.6 million, Norway's population is the Nordic nations' second smallest.

The site of the earliest human settlement in Scandinavia (before 8000 B.C.), Norway was ruled by Denmark for almost four centuries, until 1814. Reluctantly joining with Sweden after the Napoleonic wars, Norway coveted independence, which it did not achieve entirely until 1905, when it became the constitutional monarchy that it remains today. Eager to establish a separate national identity, the Norwegians looked for something uniquely their own, and found it by reaching back to the people they saw as their earliest forbears: the Vikings. The heroic exploits and distinctive ornamental motifs of these seafarers provided the same inspiration the *Kalevala* had offered to the Finns, a people with similarly strong craft traditions.

As the ruins uncovered at Pompeii and Herculaneum sparked revivals of classicism in France and England, so the excavation of Viking ships in the nineteenth century inspired Norwegian design. The majestic vessels and their daring masters became touchstones for national pride, initiating the Viking revival, a style that made a political statement in the country's move toward separation from Sweden. Adopting the bellicose Vikings subtly expressed the Norwegians' resentment of their political domination by others.

1-014
Scandia Chair, Hans Brattrud, 1957
Original Producer: Høve
Current Producer: Fjord Fiesta
(see also pages 99, 127)

1-014

Incorporating the distinctive ornamental motifs of the Viking ships as well as those of medieval stave churches (a classic Norwegian form that was adapted to many public buildings), the distinctive Dragon style continued into the first decades of the twentieth century, even enjoying a later revival. Art Nouveau was a congenial partner for the Viking aesthetic, softening the primitive Nordic elements and grotesque figures with its flowing, organic forms. Slow to accept modernism, the Norwegians were influenced by the Arts and Crafts movement, and later by the Art Deco style which, despite its proclaimed modernity, was rooted in traditional forms.

Norway's interest in the decorative arts is long-standing. One of the oldest decorative arts museums in Scandinavia was founded in Norway in the late nineteenth century, based on the model of London's Victoria and Albert Museum, and the Norwegian Handicrafts Society was formed in 1892. In 1900, Norway was an exhibitor at the Exposition Universelle in Paris, showing Dragon-style silver and enamelware. Four years later, Norway won a grand prize at the Louisiana Purchase Exposition in St. Louis, Missouri. More closely linked to handicrafts than its neighbors, Norway's furniture has tended to emphasize quality and utility rather than design, and the country has become more widely celebrated for its distinctive craftwork—particularly in silver—than for its furniture. As crafts were joined with industrial production, the concept of design emerged, but the ties to handicraft remain: one word for designer in Norwegian is *formgiver*, suggesting three-dimensional handmade objects rather than drawings on paper.

Despite the availability of raw materials, the furniture industry in Norway was late to develop. Craft guilds endured until the mid-nineteenth century, delaying the introduction of machine production, which arrived in the country only after World War I. Factories gradually began to replace workshops, as part of an effort to rebuild the economy during the Depression years. Norway's first training program in furniture design was established in 1939 under Professor Arne Korsmo. With few exceptions, however, Norwegian furniture has been strongly influenced by Danish models, diluting the impact—and the international attention—given to skilled Norwegian designers such as Alf Sture and Ingmar Relling.

The Norwegians have always been interested in their homes. Living in relatively larger spaces than their Nordic neighbors, they characteristically spend a large proportion of their incomes on decorating and redecorating. As a result, most furniture production, even in recent times, has been for domestic rather than commercial use. Lacking a class of nobles with grand manor houses such as those in Sweden, Norwegian design has concentrated on simple objects rather than luxurious ones. Most Norwegian furniture has an egalitarian air, reflecting a focus on honesty of materials, simplicity of detail, function, accessibility, and craftsmanship. This emphasis on quality and practicality rather than on distinctive design may explain Norway's failure to produce "name" designers like those in other Nordic countries.

Norway, though attempting to remain neutral, was invaded and occupied by Germany during World War II. After the Nazi's infamous "scorched earth" retreat, which destroyed buildings and bridges in its path, Norway had to rebuild its industry virtually from scratch. Focusing on economic recovery rather than aesthetics, Norwegian design had in effect to begin anew. A wave of new homebuilding in the 1950s spurred two decades of growth in the furniture industry, which employed as many workers as all other industries in the country combined. Most production copied Continental European styles, and even when furniture manufacturers began to offer scholarships to architects studying furniture design, modernism was slow to gain ground. Though Norway participated with its neighbors in many of the mid-century joint exhibitions and cooperative marketing efforts, most of the objects shown were along traditional lines, and Norway was less closely associated with the image of Scandinavian modern than were Denmark, Sweden, or Finland.

Although a Norwegian developed the production process for expandable polystyrene (patented as Styropor), enabling such celebrated modern designs as the chairs of Denmark's Arne Jacobsen, it was the development of the contract market—products for office and commercial installations—that stimulated innovation in Norwegian furniture, by designers such as Sven Ivar Dysthe and Peter Opsvik. Hoping to encourage more adventurous design, the Norwegian Design Council began a program of annual awards in 1963 and since 1974 has been working to match designers with manufacturers.

The discovery of oil in the late 1960s enriched and then dominated the Norwegian economy, to the detriment of all other industries, including furniture. Petrochemical industries drove the commerce: exports of oil were far more profitable than those of household goods, and it was easier to purchase design than to nurture its development. Designers left the industry, many factories closed, and design lay fallow. Today, much of the furniture sold in Norway is actually produced elsewhere.

Fortunately for the future of Norwegian design, this short-sighted attitude began to change late in the twentieth century. Norwegian pride was reawakened by the 1994 Lillehammer Olympic Games' extraordinarily successful graphic identity program, which verified the value of design as a means of promoting national identity. Since then, government efforts have joined private corporations in focusing on the need to develop design as a marketable asset, particularly looking ahead to the possibility of diminished oil reserves. There are now two strong programs of furniture design, in Oslo and Bergen. And at the Norwegian University of Science and Technology (NTNU), the concept of design management is being used in an innovative educational program geared to designing for industry. A sophisticated new generation of designers has sparked an interest in fresh and creative ideas. Design, in furniture and other industrial goods, promises to become an increasingly essential export for Norway in the years to come.

SWEDEN

Forming the eastern part of the Scandinavian peninsula, Sweden is the fourth largest country in Europe and the largest of the Nordic nations (450,000 square kilometers—about 175,000 square miles). It is also the most industrialized. Rich in natural resources, it boasts a varied geography of mountains, forests, rivers, and lakes. Sweden is a prosperous nation with a diverse population of more than nine million, many of whose ancestors immigrated from elsewhere. It is known for its strong welfare elements, and largely as a result of political neutrality has been spared the historic deprivations and disruptions of most of its neighbors. Sweden is tied to both Denmark and Norway by their linked Germanic-based languages, which facilitate communication among them and form one basis of their shared Scandinavianism.

The other basis was the Kalmar Union, in which Sweden joined with Denmark and Norway under a single ruler between the late fourteenth and early sixteenth centuries. Factions in Sweden opposed the dominance of Denmark, however, and the coalition ended when Gustavus I came to the throne of Sweden in 1523. By the seventeenth century, Sweden had become the most powerful of the Nordic nations, an absolute monarchy, and a participant in both the Thirty Years' War and the Napoleonic wars (at different times gaining dominance over Finland and its sometime ally, Norway). Since 1809, it has been a peaceful constitutional monarchy, preserving its neutrality through two world wars. During the twentieth century, liberal reforms transformed Sweden into a social democracy and a thriving modern welfare state.

The country has a homogeneous and flourishing design tradition, though one that was for some time strongly influenced by Europe—mostly French and then German styles. First Baroque and Rococo, then Neoclassical and Empire, and later Jugendstil adaptations prevailed until well into the nineteenth century, when Sweden began to develop its own design aesthetic. Like Denmark accustomed to independence, Sweden has not been driven to seek expressions of a national identity, and its design is less a reflection of patriotism than of social and humanistic concerns.

The seeds of modernism in Sweden, as in the rest of the western world, were sown in the nineteenth century, though they emerged a bit later than those in Continental Europe. The Swedish Society for Industrial Design (founded in 1845) sought to elevate standards of design, and the Swedish Domestic Crafts Association (1894) supported artistic craftwork. But the most influential changes came after 1899, when Ellen Key, a writer and social reformer, published a pamphlet, *Skönhet för Alla* (Beauty for All), a bold idea in the elitist Victorian age. Key laid the ideological foundation for Swedish—and indeed all Scandinavian—modernism. She believed that everyone has the right to enjoy beauty. Linking the short summers and long dark Swedish winters to a taste for happy colors, air, and light, she was probably inspired, at least in part, by paintings by Carl Larsson in Stockholm's 1897 Exhibition of Art and Industry. Larsson's watercolors of his home, published in 1899, visualized a uniquely Swedish form of modernism—an appealing country style with rustic furniture, light-toned woods, and colors drawn from nature—warm blues, sunny yellows, soft greens. Based on folk tradition, Larsson's style and the Swedish interiors it inspired reflect the influence of English Arts and Crafts.

The Industrial Art Exhibition in Stockholm in 1909 showed the work of modern designer–craftsmen, but the new aesthetic did not take hold immediately. Industrial art at the Baltic Exhibition in Malmö was indifferently received by critics, though Swedish textile arts were praised. In 1917, however, at Stockholm's Home Exhibition, architect Gunnar Asplund and furniture designer Carl Malmsten pioneered a new direction with a series of clean-lined interiors intended for the working class.

In 1919, writer and critic Gregor Paulsson published *Vaackrare Vardagsvara* (More Beautiful Things for Everyday Use), extending Key's ideas to call for cooperation between craft and industry, looking to the Deutscher Werkbund (German Work Federation) as a model. His ideas were similar to those expressed by Walter Gropius in the Bauhaus Manifesto and practiced in the legendary school, established in Weimar Germany in 1919 and closed by the Nazis in 1933. The Bauhaus sought to reunite the fine arts and craft, and its student-designed products were intended for mass production, though most were made by hand in the school's workshops. Paulsson, however, helped bring theory into practice by calling for manufacturers to enlist artists to design their products. Orrefors, a producer of fine handblown glass, was the first to respond, hiring painters Simon Gate and Edvin Hald, who created objects that brought international acclaim for Swedish design. At the 1925 Exposition Internationale des Arts Décoratifs et Industriels Modernes in Paris, the Swedes won thirty-five Grands Prix and many other awards, prompting the coining of the phrase "Swedish Grace" by English journalist Morton Shand. The Exposition was a milestone for Sweden, bringing it considerable prestige and indirectly benefiting its neighbors as well. It is perhaps anachronistic that Scandinavian design, celebrated for its accessibility and egalitarian qualities, was first brought to international attention by luxury products affordable only to an affluent clientele.

This narrow focus broadened after the 1930 Stockholm Exhibition, when Gunnar Asplund's move to functionalism initiated considerable controversy, but stimulated the development of modern products designed for a wider public. Functionalism, which placed utility above all other concerns, including that of aesthetics, was not widely adopted in

1-015

1-015
Armchair, Erik Gunnar Asplund, 1930
Producer, Källemo (since 1980)

1-016
Eva Chair, Bruno Mathsson, c.1941
Original Producer: Karl Mathsson,
later Dux
Current Producer: Mathsson International
www.Jacksons.se

1-016

Sweden but served as a catalyst for change, which then progressed rapidly. In the early 1930s Bruno Mathsson designed furniture in laminated bentwood, paralleling the work of Alvar Aalto in Finland. At the 1937 Exhibition Internationale des Arts et Techniques de la Vie Moderne in Paris, interiors by Josef Frank, an expatriate Austrian and member of the Wiener Werkstatte (Vienna Workshop) hired by Swedish firm Svenskt Tenn, were clearly modernist, and by 1938 a "Swedish Modern" promotion was staged by the Lord & Taylor department store in New York City, presaging the wave of Scandinavian design that would dominate the years just after World War II.

At the 1939 New York World's Fair, the Swedish pavilion by Svend-Erik Markelius presented an exhibit entitled "Swedish Modern: A Movement Towards Sanity in Design." The title deftly summed up the country's approach to modern design, one that emphasized simplicity and practicality. As Danish furniture characteristically emphasized cabinetry skills, Swedish furniture tended to focus on technical solutions to design problems. In the 1940s, the Swedes developed a system of universal measurements that anticipated ergonomics, and in 1944 introduced what was probably the first K-D chair (by Elias Svedberg for Nardisha Kompaniet). Combining high-tech and humanism, the commonsense approach of the Swedes eschewed the inflexible standards often associated with modernism; their respect for art and technology brought craft and industry together instead of preserving the conflict between them.

Despite the fact that Sweden generated the philosophy that was the source of Scandinavian modernism, its furniture did not gain the international celebrity awarded to Danish style in postwar years. This was caused in part by a lack of aggressive marketing, but it is also attributable to the subtlety of Swedish design: Swedish furniture is generally simpler than its Danish or Finnish counterparts. It is, however, consistently appealing. Most of it is made of native woods, beech, birch, and oak, which replaced the darker and more formal ones of European-inspired design. Swedish textiles have achieved their own identity, with floral prints and lively colors reflecting the continuing legacy of Carl Larsson and Josef Frank. This is evident in the continuing appeal of Swedish country and Gustavian styles.

Considering the Swedish interest in technology, Swedish industrial design has understandably flourished in the past several decades, as the country took the lead in developing innovative products in communications, health care, household equipment, and other manufactured goods. This has generated new interest in all areas of design, including furniture. IKEA, founded in Sweden in 1943 (though its first store did not open until 1958) and expanding exponentially in the last quarter of the twentieth century, has been a considerable factor in stimulating that interest. Despite its offerings of inexpensive furniture focused on good looks rather than long-term durability, IKEA has strengthened the association of Sweden with user-friendly, practical, and affordable products, and has made an international market receptive to other designs from the same country.

In the past two decades, many Swedish furniture factories have closed, and rising domestic production costs have led others to relocate manufacturing facilities overseas. At the same time, however, availability of sophisticated materials, new technologies, and concerns about the environment and sustainability have made professional designers more essential to the industry. With increasing awareness of design potential to enhance the country's international prestige, innovation is now being spearheaded both by established producers and new, smaller firms, as well as by young designers who have brought new flair and originality to Swedish furniture.

I-017

I-017
Side Chair, Josef Frank, 1947
Producer: Svenskt Tenn
www.Jacksons.se

THE POSTWAR DECADES
1950–1965

These were the Golden Years, when Scandinavian design exploded to prominence throughout the West. The propellants were not only its appealing, accessible design but also the convergence of political circumstances, the vagaries of fashion, and perhaps most important, astute marketing on the part of governments, trade associations, and forward-thinking importers and retailers. Though Swedish and Danish furniture had been exhibited in American venues as early as the 1920s, its exposure was limited. It was not until the late 1940s that Scandinavian furniture moved aggressively into export markets. It would dominate them for much of the next two decades.

In the years following World War II, the Nordic countries—which, except for Norway, were spared the devastation and impoverishment suffered by their European neighbors—were well positioned to begin developing export markets for their furniture. As the western world began to embrace modernism, the Scandinavian aesthetic was more welcoming and easier to accept than that of the avant-garde of Germany. In addition to the severity of the designs, the association with Nazism hindered products from that country. (As it happened, by this time, the leading designers and artists of Germany and other European countries had fled, some of the most important of them to the United States, where they would nurture a generation of American modernists.) Scandinavian design, in contrast, was free of unpleasant connections, and the objects themselves reflected the humanity and love of craft shared by the Nordic nations. Moreover, the Scandinavian approach to functionalism—including furniture that could expand, stack, fold, or nest—was invitingly user-friendly, and comfortable as well as practical.

During this period, a new image was encouraged by the Nordic Council, which had been established in 1948 to help promote industry in the difficult postwar years and in which all Nordic countries except Iceland participated. The concept of Scandinavian design was, to a great degree, the result of the council's efforts to promulgate the myth of a common culture and a single aesthetic, blending national images in an innovative joint propaganda effort. The results were an unprecedented success that, while erasing the countries' individualities, enhanced them all. The term *Scandinavian design*, used in 1951 in London and Paris, became internationally recognized after a celebrated exhibition in America a few years later.

The characteristics of Scandinavian design—its use of natural materials, lightness of weight and scale, understatement, simplicity, and respect for handicraft and tradition—were emphasized as the logical outgrowth of the egalitarian, socially conscious, and humanitarian societies from which they emerged. The marriage of crafts and industry, which had been sought by design reformers and critics for a century, had finally been achieved.

Although the Scandinavian image was an umbrella covering all of the Nordic countries, its benefits were not uniform. When it came to furniture, Denmark overwhelmed its neighbors, and the term *Danish modern* came to designate the best of the genre. Developments such as modular and stacking storage, shelf systems, and K-D furniture fueled the interest in and the demand for such products from all of the Nordic nations.

In 1951, the first postwar edition of the prestigious Triennale di Milano provided a triumphant showcase for products from the Nordic nations and was a breakthrough for Scandinavian design. With an exhibition designed by Tapio Wirkkala, Finland took home more awards (thirty-two) than any other country; Denmark's Hans Wegner garnered a Grand Prix for his Round Chair; and Finn Juhl's furniture designs were also honored, in a series of individual successes that garnered benefits for all. The Finnish triumph led to a traveling exhibition, Modern Art in Finland, staged by the Victoria and Albert Museum in London, in 1952, and in that year the Smithsonian

1-018

1-019

Opposite
1-018
Round Chair, Hans J. Wegner, 1949
Cabinetmaker: Johannes Hansen
Producer: PP Møbler
www.Jacksons.se
(see also page 72)

1-019
Laminated Chair and Table, Grete Jalck, 1963
Producer: Poul Jeppesen
Not in current production
www.Jacksons.se

This page
1-020
Sideboard, Hans J. Wegner, 1950
Producer: Ry Møbler
Not in current production
www.Jacksons.se

1-021
Sofa, Borge Mogensen, 1960s
Producer: Fredericia
www.Jacksons.se

1-020

1-021

Institution in Washington, D.C., sponsored the exhibition, Finnish Arts and Crafts, which traveled to thirteen American cities.

At the 1954 Triennale, another triumph for Finland, prizes were also awarded to Denmark and Sweden for modern ceramics and glass, and to Norway for Viking-inspired Dragon-style silver; in its fair debut, Norway had chosen to present its own distinctive aesthetic. The Finns in particular would continue to make strong presentations at Triennale events in 1957, 1960, and 1963.

The American media enthusiastically embraced Scandinavian design. The magazine *Interiors* featured on a 1950 cover the Wegner Round Chair it dubbed "The Chair," and in 1951 *House Beautiful* gave similar expo-

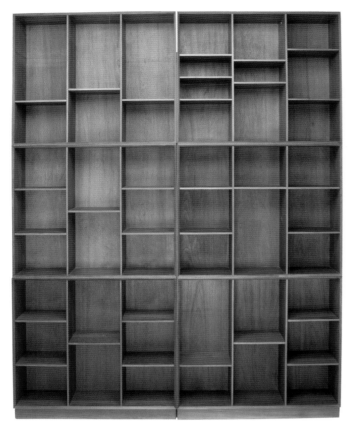

I-022

I-023

sure to a Wirkkala leaf platter, citing it as the year's "most beautiful object." The following year, the film *Hans Christian Andersen*, a musical starring the multitalented Danny Kaye, captivated American audiences with a fairytale impression of Copenhagen and the Danes.

Notwithstanding these successes, the Scandinavian image in America is most often traced to a single event: Design in Scandinavia, an exhibition that opened in January 1954 at the Virginia Museum of Fine Arts and subsequently traveled to two dozen museums in the United States and Canada over a period of three-and-a-half years. The exhibition was a cooperative effort by the governments and crafts associations of Denmark, Finland, Norway, and Sweden and featured seven hundred objects. The displays included Danish furniture, silver, and porcelain; Swedish glass; Norwegian crafts and woven goods; and Finnish rugs. Drawing almost a million visitors, the show received substantial publicity in magazines and newspapers. It presented the countries as a group, stressing their common design characteristics and furthering the notion of a single Scandinavian style. A parallel exhibition at the Georg Jensen store in New York City, Scandinavian Design in Use, featured furniture by Alvar Aalto, Bruno Mathsson, and Hans Wegner, offering the objects for sale. In an interesting cultural crossover, an exhibition of American design was sent in 1954 to tour Denmark and Norway. It was called American Form—the word "design"

I-022
Stacking Shelves, Hvidt/Molgaard-
Nielsen, 1950s
Producer: unknown, Danish
Not in current production
www.Jacksons.se

I-023
Stacking Chair, Axel Larsson, 1950
Producer: unknown, Swedish
Not in current production
www.Jacksons.se

was not yet not in common use by the practical-minded Scandinavians. It has been suggested that this exhibition helped to shape the Scandinavian aesthetic to complement informal American lifestyles.

Scandinavian furniture was included in virtually every major design exhibition of the time. In New York, the Museum of Modern Art's series of Good Design exhibitions, mounted from 1950 to 1955, highlighted a number of Danish objects, as well as furniture by Alvar Aalto. Finn Juhl designed the 1951 exhibition. Edgar Kaufmann jr., the influential curator of design at MoMA, was a key player in awakening Americans to Scandinavian design. As early as 1948 he had written a major article about Finn Juhl for *Interiors* magazine, and he continued to write about Scandinavian design, and Danish design specifically. Kaufmann helped contact museums on behalf of the Design in Scandinavia exhibit and was instrumental in arranging for Finn Juhl to design a line for Baker Furniture in 1951. (A decade earlier, furniture by Danish émigré Jens Risom for Knoll had been

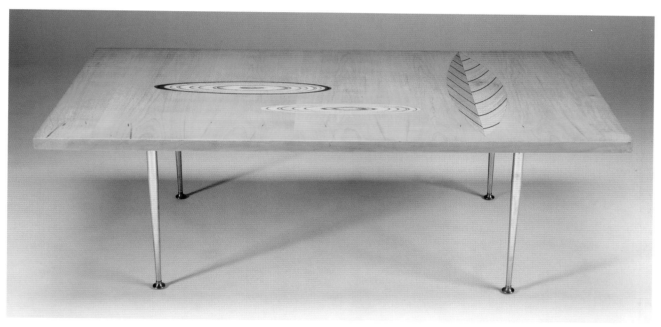

I-024

I-024
Coffee Table, Tapio Wirkkala, 1950
Producer: Asko
Not in current production
www.Jacksons.se

the first translations of a Danish furniture aesthetic for an American producer.)

In addition to international fairs, events within the Nordic countries began to draw attention from abroad. In 1955, the H55 fair in the port city of Helsingborg (on the twenty-fifth anniversary of the historic Stockholm Exhibition) presented Sweden's new approach to modernism, focusing on practical, everyday objects. The Scandinavia Furniture Fair, a modest event in Fredericia, Denmark, began to assume greater importance, and by 1966 moved to a new home, the glass-enclosed Bella Centre exhibition hall outside Copenhagen. Here the best of the new Scandinavian furniture was introduced each May to a growing and

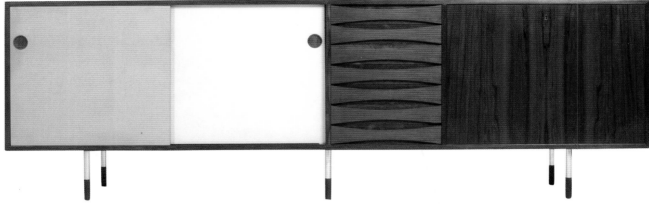

1-025

increasingly international audience. Most of the
exhibitors were Danish, but Denmark's furniture
industry was by far the Nordic countries' largest, con-
sisting of some three hundred firms. Although the
most innovative designs were at the high end of the
market, the majority of the furniture shown was relatively mid-range in price and appropriate for export.

Furniture by Finland's Alvar Aalto and Sweden's
Bruno Mathsson had been available in the United
States since the 1930s, but relatively few Americans
had been exposed to Scandinavian design except for
those traveling abroad. A few pioneering importers
helped to change that. Austrian émigré Georg
Tanier began importing furniture from Sweden in
1946, and introduced Danish modern furniture to
America in 1952; Charles Stendig imported Asko
and then other Finnish furniture beginning in
1954; and others followed. Irving Richards and
Charles Morgenthau imported accessories through
Raymor, and Ted Nierenberg's Dansk Designs marketed
Jens Quistgaard's teak servingware, tableware, and cookware.

By the 1950s, cutting-edge retailers were beginning to feature
Scandinavian furniture. Design Research in Cambridge, Massachusetts,
Scandinavian Design in Boston, Frank Brothers in Long Beach, California,
and Watson and Boehler in Chicago were among the pathbreakers. By the
1960s others, such as Workbench and Maurice Villency in New York and
SCAN in Washington, D.C., were offering affordably priced furniture
from Scandinavian producers along with other contemporary designs, and
retailers such as Crate and Barrel and Pottery Barn sold complementary
tableware and accessories. By that time, dozens of Scandinavian specialty
stores had opened in and around major cities, primarily in the Northeast
and mostly owned by Danish expatriates. (The majority of these shifted

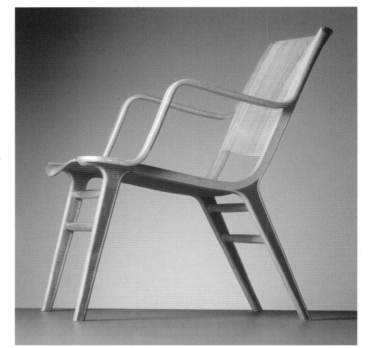

1-026

1-025
Sideboard, Arne Vodder, 1959
Producer: Sibast
Not in current production
www.Jacksons.se

1-026
AX Chair, Hvidt/Molgaard-Nielsen, 1947
Producer: unknown, Swedish
Not in current production

focus or closed altogether after interest in Scandinavian design flagged in the 1970s.) The Georg Jensen store on Fifth Avenue in New York turned over a full floor to furniture, and initiated the Lunning Prize, a prestigious award program that recognized young designers—two each year—from the Nordic countries. The program brought increased attention to Nordic design in all areas, until it ended in 1970.

Major department stores took note. Bloomingdale's, in 1958, staged the first of what would become an influential tradition of import fairs, "At Home with Scandinavian Design," with room settings outfitted in Scandinavian style and a variety of Scandinavian products specially imported for the occasion. Other stores held similar events. Most of the furniture shown was Danish—a considerable boost to the Danish export market, which doubled its sales to the United States in the next decade.

1-027

1-027
Drop-leaf Table, Bruno Mathsson, 1950s
Producer: Karl Mathsson
(Photo courtesy Wright/Brian Franczyk Photography)

As international travel became more affordable, the Nordic countries promoted their products to a growing tourist trade. The Scandinavian Design Cavalcade in summer and fall of 1956 showed a wide range of products from all but Iceland in a series of exhibitions and events in Stockholm, Copenhagen, Oslo, and Helsinki, including tours to factories and workshops.

The enthusiasm continued into the next decade, when in New York City the Metropolitan Museum of Art staged an Arts of Denmark: Viking to Modern exhibition in 1960 and the Cooper-Hewitt Museum in 1962 opened Creative Craft in Denmark. Iceland, finally entering the field, opened an Icelandic Arts and Crafts Shop in New York to show textiles and furniture designs. Finland, which continued to shine at the Triennale, was honored by a Finlandia exhibition at the Victoria and Albert Museum in London.

1-028

1-029

As late as 1964, twelve of the fifteen model rooms featured in Bloomingdale's semiannual furniture event were described by the *New York Times* as having a "Danish flavor." The Nordic nations, with Denmark in the lead, had effectively created a "brand identity" with design, building on the premise stated by a Danish journalist who, in 1961, wrote that, "Industrial art is to Scandinavia what painting is to France, music to Germany, and the Alps to Switzerland."

Throughout this time, the growing reputation of Nordic design was celebrated in two influential Danish-based publications: *Mobilia* (1955–84) and *Design from Scandinavia* (begun in 1967 and still flourishing). Both featured new designs in a variety of media and, circulated internationally, gave further impetus to growing sales of the products shown and others from the same sources.

Toward the end of the period, several factors led to a shift in the marketplace and to a movement away from Scandinavian design. Fashion, as always, demanded change, and the modesty and timelessness of Scandinavian furniture—particularly the Danish styles that had dominated the field—became drawbacks rather than advantages. In 1963 Finn

1-028
Cone Chair, Verner Panton, 1958
Producer: Plus-Linje
Not in current production
www.Jacksons.se

1-029
Ant Chair, Arne Jacobsen, 1952
Producer: Fritz Hansen
www.Jacksons.se
(see also page 68)

Opposite
1-030
34622 Chest of Drawers, Josef Frank, 1930s
Producer: Svenskt Tenn
www.Jacksons.se
(see also page 255)

1-030

1-031

1-032

Juhl told a *New York Times* reporter that design in the Nordic countries had become "but a refinement and continuing of what has been already." A few designers, such as Danes Arne Jacobsen and Werner Panton, were beginning to explore new forms and new materials. But for the most part, Scandinavian design was perceived as steady, reliable, and, ultimately, unexciting.

1965–1980

By 1968, when *House Beautiful* devoted an entire issue to a celebration of Scandinavian design, the designation, and the style, had already peaked, and a new wave of avant-garde furniture was being developed by idiosyncratic Italian designers. The Italians captured the collective imagination of the media and marketplace with their witty and unconventional—though not necessarily practical—designs. The Scandinavians, confident of the timelessness and commonsense qualities of their furniture, were slow to respond to the shift of fashion, and continued to offer variations of the styles that had brought them success. According to government figures, the United States accounted for almost 20 percent of Danish furniture exports in 1973; by the end of the decade, this had begun to shrink dramatically.

The 1970s and 1980s were stressful times for young Nordic designers, who labored under the weight of the reputations of their celebrated predecessors, many of whom were still alive and still designing. Iconic names such as Aalto, Jacobsen, Juhl, Mathsson, and Wegner, once inspirational, became intimidating to those who might have been tempted to explore

1-033

1-031
Lamino Chair, Yngve Ekström, 1956
Producer: Swedese (reintroduced 2003)
(see also page 109)

1-032
Siesta Lounge, Ingmar Relling, 1965
Producer: Westnofa

1-033
INKA Chair, Gunnar Magnusson, 1960
Collection: Museum of Design/Applied Art, Iceland

new horizons. Though crafts were enjoying a revival, they had little influence on production furniture, in which Scandinavian design initiative was faltering. Young designers of the 1970s "anti-design" movements tried to distance themselves from the limitations of Scandinavian modernism, with experimental, unconventional designs, but their efforts were not influential enough to reverse the decline in creativity. As Kerstin Wickman, professor of design history at Stockholm's Konstfack University has noted, "After the turbulent 1960s and early 1970s, the Nordic design world ran out of steam."

There were exceptions. In 1973, Iceland had its first export success with Pétur Lúthersson's Stacco chair: 200,000 pieces were sold. From Sweden, Johan Huldt and Jan Dranger melded Bauhaus form and pop colors in tubular metal "Innovator" seating that topped one million in sales. Finland's Muurame factory made its mark with sophisticated but

1-035

1-034
Balans Activ, Peter Opsvik, 1984 (original design 1979)
Producer: Håg, Stokke (many variations)
(see aso pages 202, 203)

1-035
Karuselli Chair, Yrjö Kukkapuro, 1964
Producer: Avarte
(see also page 102)

practical children's furniture and light-scaled modular storage pieces; Yrjo Kukkapuro and Eero Aarnio, meanwhile, experimented with color and form in furniture. The unique "Balans" seating concept was developed in Norway by Hans Christian Mengshoel and applied by Peter Opsvik. Scandinavian producers showed these and other attractive new designs at the international fairs, but originality, for the most part, was dormant.

Economic factors also affected the changing climate of design. In the 1970s, capital investment—particularly in Finland and Sweden—began to

1-036

shift toward high technology. The focus in Norway moved to oil, and to manufacturing of products related to the petroleum industry. As a result, furniture production suffered, and many factories closed. In Sweden, the focus on industrial design produced a variety of sophisticated, innovative products, but little innovative furniture. The interest was in rational, practical objects, many dealing with challenges of disabilities and health-care considerations. In Denmark, promotion budgets for the furniture industry were severely cut, on the erroneous assumption that past performance would assure continued success.

A bright spot, however, would help to reinvigorate the Scandinavian furniture industry. The postwar boom in office and hotel construction in most urban areas, and particularly in Finland, created a new market for the use of furniture in commercial interiors. This led to the development of a contract furniture industry, as it had in the United States. Established manufacturers introduced collections for this purpose, and a number of new firms formed to meet the growing demand; most of the expansion

1-036
Ball Chair, Eero Aarnio, 1966
Producer: Asko
Not in current production

1-037
Stacco Chair, Pétur Lúthersson, 1980
Producer: GKS

1-038
Sofa, Huldt & Dranger, 1983
Producer: Innovator
Not in current production

1-039

1-039
Planet Chair, Sven Ivar Dysthe, 1965
Producers: Stokke, Fora Form
(see also page 92)

1-040
"Bucky" Stool, Einar Thorsteinn
Asgeirsson, 1980
Collection: Museum of Design/
Applied Art, Iceland

1-041
Lounge Chair, Fredrik Kayser, 1968
Producer: Vatne
Not in current production

in the Scandinavian furniture industry in these and succeeding decades
has come from products developed for corporate and so-called hospitality
installations. Many of the designs have proved appropriate for residential
interiors as well.

In 1970, the Danish consulate staged a traveling exhibition, An American Inspiration:
Danish Modern and Shaker Design,
which opened in Boston. It suggested a new direction in residential
furniture: a move away from the
teak-rosewood-walnut formula and
earth-tone color schemes that had
defined the image of Scandinavian
design, to paler woods and a fresh
new look. It presaged a more open-
minded attitude and reinvigorated
creativity on the part of both the Nordic
designers and the producers on whom they relied.

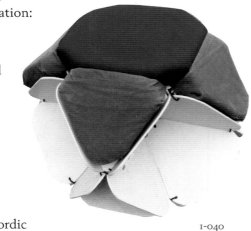

1-040

1-041

1-042

1-042
Oscar Chair, Harri Korhonen, 1980
Producer: Inno

1-043
Experiment, Yrjö Kukkapuro
Producer: Avarte

Not in current production

1-044
Tabouret, Aagard Andersen, 1980
Producer: PP Møbler

1-045
Barstool, Börge Lindau and Bo Lindecrantz,
1968
Producer: Lammhults
(see also page 202)

1-043

1-044

1-045

1980–2000

In August, 1980, a *New York Times* article by architecture critic Ada Louise Huxtable bemoaned "The Melancholy Fate of Danish Modern Style," asking "Whatever happened to Danish modern . . . a tidal wave of good taste and good design in the 1950s?", and answering that it had been supplanted by other styles. The decline, the *Times* reported, was in part attributable to inferior mass-produced copies that cheapened the Danish (read *Scandinavian*) furniture image. Though this was certainly true, some of the fault lay with conservative Nordic designers and short-sighted manufacturers who had been introducing virtually the same products year after year. Another contributing factor was the introduction into the market of low-priced, low-quality furniture, some made in overseas production facilities for Nordic manufacturers (to avoid increasing labor costs at home), and some by other countries attempting to piggyback on the popularity of Scandinavian design.

Uncomfortably aware of their faded image, the Danes and their neighbors aggressively sought to reawaken interest in Scandinavian design, and to encourage the development of designs that would recapture their place in the international market.

Scandinavia Today in 1982–83 was a fifteen-month celebration of art and culture staged in museums and institutions in New York City. Hosted by Scandinavian royalty as well as industry representatives, it included exhibitions and events intended to raise the profile of the Nordic countries, capitalizing on both an invigorated design community and a strong dollar that encouraged imports.

Its most influential element was an exhibition, Scandinavian Modern Design: 1880–1980, which opened in September 1982 at the Cooper-Hewitt Museum, chronicling a century of design in all media in the Nordic countries. The companion publication, edited by David Revere McFadden, was the first major American study of the subject, and though it continued to promulgate the myth of design unity, it gave a considerable boost to Scandinavian design's identity. The exhibition subsequently traveled to St. Paul, Minnesota, Washington, D.C., and London, and the project, proving again the benefits of all-Nordic cooperation, generated considerable press and public attention.

During the same period Finland enjoyed some high-profile exposure of its own: Finland: Nature, Design, and Architecture toured American venues from 1981 to 1983; Cooper-Hewitt staged an exhibition of Finnish glass in 1985; and as the century drew to a close, in 1998 the

1-046

1-046
Concrete Chair, Jonas Bohlin, 1980
Producer: Källemo
(see also page 70)

Museum of Modern Art celebrated the centenary of Alvar Aalto's birth with an exhibition of his architecture.

In 1983 Sweden's Svensk Form design organization initiated an annual competition, Good Swedish Form, to stimulate the development of well-designed products in categories including furniture, industrial design and, later, graphics and communication design. In 1980, *Form Function Finland* was launched to provide a public forum for Finnish design, reporting on developments in all disciplines, and in 1989 Design Forum Finland established the Pro Finnish Design Award, fostering cooperation between industry and designers by awarding businesses that encouraged good design. A new international version of the Georg Jensen prize was instituted in 1987, and the Danish Furniture Manufacturers Association undertook a promotion program aimed at reestablishing their preeminent position by calling attention to new designs.

In 1985 Bloomingdale's staged Style Scandinavia, showcasing design from all five Nordic nations. The show echoed the store's 1958 promotion, again putting its imprimatur on the genre and presenting it to a new generation of consumers. At the furniture market in High Point, North Carolina, some American producers cited Scandinavian design as inspiration for their new collections. And that year Sweden's IKEA opened its first store in America, presaging what would become a phenomenon of marketing savvy and a catalyst for the revival of interest in Scandinavian design.

I-047

In 1986, however, a precipitous drop in the dollar cut the exchange rate almost in half; while the dollar before could buy twelve Danish kroner, for example, it could now buy only six. Though affecting all imported goods, the shrunken dollar particularly harmed U.S. sales of Scandinavian furniture which, notwithstanding its superior quality and design, and its costly iconic objects, had been mostly priced in the middle range of the market. High prices, to consumers, were not acceptable for simple, unpretentious furniture. Hoping to overcome resistance in an increasingly competitive marketplace, the sponsors of the Scandinavian Furniture Fair in Copenhagen undertook a promotion program from 1984 to 1987 to build international attendance, and specifically to attract retailers beyond the narrow market of Scandinavian specialty stores that had been its primary outlets.

Slowly but steadily, the situation began to improve. While many of the established designers remained active, a new generation had emerged to rebel against the tyranny of formulaic design. Awakened to the need for change, manufacturers became more receptive to furniture that required investment in new materials and technology. As handcrafting techniques

I-047
Collapsible Table, Niels Jørgen Haugesen, 1984
Producer: Fredericia
(see also page 221)

Opposite
I-048
8000 Series Stools, Johnny Sørensen and Rud Thygesen, 1978
Producer: Magnus Olesen
(see also page 276)

I-049
Planka, Lindau & Lindecrantz, 1986
Producer: Lammhults
(see also page 264)

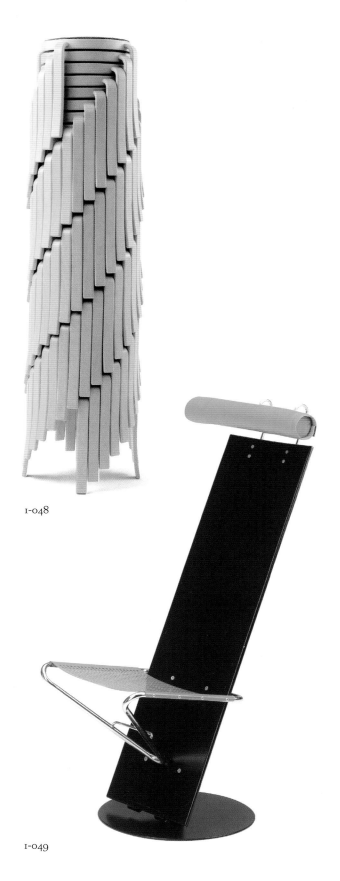

1-048

1-049

were supplanted by machine production, some qualities were lost (particularly with the end of the Danish Cabinetmaker's Guild Exhibitions that had generated the most celebrated Danish designs), but innovation developed in other ways. Designers showed that a more venturesome approach, using less conventional forms and livelier colors, could produce furniture that was visually arresting without sacrificing either quality or function.

The 1980s saw the introduction of countless ideas in chairs, particularly stacking examples, as well as flexible storage systems, experiments with tubular metal, and user-friendly designs for the young, the sick, and the elderly. Toward the end of the decade, modular and linked seating for public spaces, executive office designs, geometric configurations of tables, and the use of new plastics and varied woods, most of them light-hued, brought a new look and new life to Scandinavian furniture. The familiar unfinished woods were often enhanced with lacquer finishes—not the high-gloss applications seen in Italian furniture, but matte or semi-gloss surfaces in muted colors and a great deal of white. A brighter palette replaced the neutrals and earth tones that had defined classic Scandinavian style, and upholstered furniture, though still light-scaled and linear, grew noticeably softer and more rounded. Modular and multipurpose furniture (a continuing preoccupation of the space-poor Scandinavians) became even more varied, and steel and aluminum frames, legs, and bases became acceptable in seating that, attractively styled, could easily suit either office or home. *Ergonomics* became a familiar term, and a necessary component of seating—office chairs, in particular, were adjustable to accommodate individual body size and weight, ensuring both comfort and good posture.

With a few exceptions, new, smaller companies took the lead in producing the most inventive designs. Kallëmo, Blå Station, and Offecct in Sweden, and Avarte and Vivero in Finland were among the innovators. Established firms like Lammhults and Swedese (Sweden), Fritz Hansen and Fredericia (Denmark), and Stokke (Norway) became increasingly varied in their product introductions. Young

1-050   1-051

designers like Thomas Sandell, Mats Theselius, Jonas Bohlin, Stefan
Lindfors, Rud Thygesen, and Johnny Sorensen and others began to figure
on the international stage. Later, promotional groups like the collective
Swecode, Sweden Next, and Danish Avantgarde Design were formed to
market new furniture abroad, sharing space and costs at major international fairs.

   Not all of the Nordic countries pursued exactly the same directions.
Danish furniture producers introduced bold and linear silhouettes direct-
ed to the contract market; Sweden focused on engineering, painted furniture, quick-assembly and modular designs; Norway explored new seating
concepts; and Finland drew attention—and admiration—with fresh ideas
in furniture that made use of new materials and lively colors, creating a
new identity for Finnish avant-garde design. Even Iceland began taking
tentative steps to join its colleagues, with individual designers producing
and even marketing their own designs.

   The increasing variety of styles and materials had one significant and
unanticipated result: Nordic furniture departed from what had been
recognized as the hallmark "Scandinavian look." This was both an advantage and a drawback, since it could no longer capitalize as easily on the
mystique that had surrounded mid-century Nordic design. Fueled by
design change and an increasingly multinational market, with furniture
produced in many areas and a broader consumer base, the traditional
Scandinavian image began to blur. Although there were still cooperative
exhibitions and promotions—in 1990 a new exhibition, Scandinavian
Design, was staged in Malmö, Sweden, by the Scandinavian Design

1-050
Bench for Two, Nanna Ditzel, 1989
Producer: Fredericia
(see also page 211)

1-051
Tango Chair, Sigurdur Gustafsson, 1998
Producer: Källemo

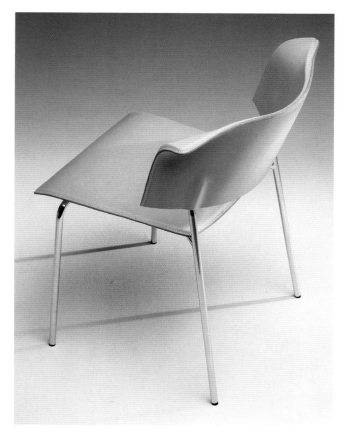

1-052

1-053

1-052
Qvintus Chair, Johannes Foersom/
Peter Hiort-Lorenzen, 1995
Producer: Lammhults
(see also page 134)

1-053
Rex Chair, Mats Theselius, 1995
Producer: Källemo

Council—the Nordic countries began to assert individual identities, and move away from stressing a single design aesthetic. At the end of 1992, for example, London's Design Museum's Festival of Scandinavian Design included three exhibits that focused on new directions in design, showing furniture from Norway, Denmark, and Sweden. On the other hand, in 1993, Norway's Norsk Form held a seminar on Scandinavian design, in which young designers expressed the desire to escape the restraints, and the connotations, of the term. And a 1999 exhibition at Amsterdam's Stedjilik Museum, The Nordic Transparency, and its accompanying publication sought to examine the issue of Scandinavian identity.

A collaborative exhibition, Design Nordic Way, visited St. Petersburg, Russia, as well as Swedish and Norwegian venues. Still another joint exhibition, staged in five European cities, showed design projects from seven different universities to illustrate the differences between the schools and the countries of origin; Iceland and Norway focused on craftsmanship and the visual arts: Finland and Sweden exhibited industrial design; and Denmark showed jewelry and ceramics.

Recognizing the potential of design as a component of the Scandinavian countries' place in the world, the Nordic governments began to provide new funding for promotion and seek new ways to harness its benefits. Reflecting this, the Scandinavian Design Council held a conference, Scandinavian Design, 1990–towards 2000, associated with

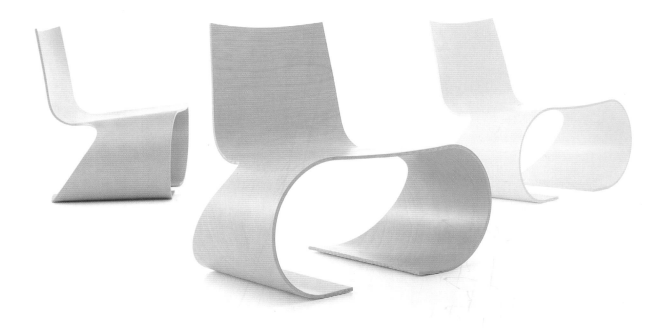

1-054

1-055

its exhibition and issued a manifesto on nature, the economy, and human needs for the future.

In the final decade of the century, Scandinavian furniture producers began to build export markets for contract furniture, a sector in which quality and good design could overcome the drawback of high price. The Danish Technological Institute made a technical breakthrough, developing a new method for bending compressed wood under heat and pressure that enabled sharper curves without breakage. An improvement on the Thonet steam processes, the environmentally-friendly technique has led to many new applications in seating and the introduction of countless numbers of slim, lightweight, and often stackable chairs from Denmark and its Nordic neighbors. In Finland, a Wood Innovation Project was introduced in 1996 to encourage new applications of the familiar material. Initially made for the domestic market, contract furniture was increasingly produced for export. Today the annual Furniture Fair in Stockholm, which outranks the Copenhagen event in

1-054
Oto Chair, Peter Karpf, 1982
(introduced 2002)
Producer: Iform
(see also page 83)

1-055
Chaise Lounge, Björn Dahlström, 2000
Producer: Dahlstrom

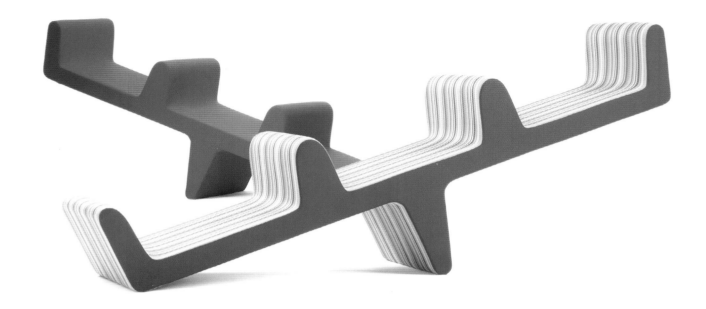

1-056

1-056
Seesaw, Louise Campbell, 2003
Producer: Erik Jørgensen
(see also page 155)

international importance, is dominated by sophisticated designs for commercial furniture.

As the century drew to a close, Sweden began a conscious effort to use design as a vehicle to promote its national identity. The success of its programs encouraged a new focus on design in all the Nordic countries. Initiatives in industrial design—and dozens of attractive and highly sophisticated products in categories like communication, engineering, light industry, and household goods—have regenerated the image of the Scandinavians as design innovators, with companies like Ericsson and Nokia contributing to shaping a new identity as forward-thinking and technically advanced.

DESIGN FOR THE TWENTY-FIRST CENTURY

In the first decade of the new century, Scandinavian design and designers have repositioned themselves to compete in a global marketplace. Without sacrificing their egalitarian roots or their compatible national traditions, they have embraced a broader view and a more inclusive aesthetic. Design is now diverse and multinational, emphasizing individual brands rather than national identities. As a result, defining today's Nordic design is problematic. Scandinavian furniture has become more varied and less obviously rooted in its traditions.

Today's young Danish designers are the third generation to practice their profession. Some of them, such as Kasper Salto, are literally the grandchildren of mid-century innovators. The majority, like designers in most countries except the United States, are multidisciplinary, working in several areas and varying media. Danish designers are less likely than their Nordic colleagues to seek training abroad, perhaps believing that they have a rich enough history from which to draw. Reverting to the old tradition of handiwork, many began as studio woodworkers to gain an understanding of how objects are made. In Sweden, designers at the prestigious Konstfack school generally spend their third year abroad, or after graduation work in other countries to acquire a broad overview of the design world. Many, such as CKR partners Mårtin Claesson, Eero Koivisto, and Ola Rune, participate in trade fairs and design for Italian and other international firms. Designing for high-profile companies, Anya Sebton, Gunilla Allard, and others have raised the visibility of women in the profession. Finnish designers, such as Sari Anttonen and Antti Kotilainen, working mostly within their own country, are increasingly looking beyond its borders. The young designers of the wittily named firm Norway Says and compatriots such as Johan Verde have brought originality to Norwegian furniture design. Icelanders such as Sigurdur Gustafsson, Elva Sólveig Oskavsdóttir, and sole practitioners marketing their own designs are contributing to the panoply of noteworthy Nordic products.

Though the cultural associations of Scandinavia remain strong, the furniture produced in these countries is no longer so easily identified by the traditional design characteristics with which it was so long associated. Metal and plastics now appear as often as wood, lively color is ubiquitous, and silhouettes are refreshingly varied as designers make freer use of curves and asymmetrical forms. Most furniture designs promoted for

1-057
Parts of a Rainbow, Christian Flindt, 2005
Producer: Flindt Design
(see also page 139)

1-057

1-058
Gubi Chair, Komplot Design, 2003
Producer: Gubi
(see also page 137)

1-059
Cloud Sofa, Märten Claesson, 2005
Producer: Swedese
(see also page 183)

export are either geared to the commercial market or intended to cross over easily from commercial to domestic use. The new look, referred to by *Form Function Finland* as "Scandi Style," merges elements of craft and industrial design. In its use of materials and technology it also reflects a concern for the environment and a sense of social responsibility that echo the humanitarian concerns of Nordic tradition.

Innovations in design education have stimulated interest in the profession, attracting increasing numbers of students to the field. The Norwegian University of Science and Technology (NTNU) in Trondheim has led the way with a program that makes partners of design and industry. In Copenhagen, the School of Architecture, the Academy of Fine Arts, and Denmark's Design School have integrated their curricula to produce more versatile and broadly skilled designers. After a steep recession in the 1990s and the loss of important markets brought about by the end of the Soviet Union, Finland has invested in design education that has helped turn around the economy and reinvigorated furniture design. Helsinki's University of Art & Design (UIAH) also sponsors international conferences to foster dialogues about design—and maintain Finland's image for design innovation.

At home and abroad, museum exhibitions are once more showcasing Nordic design. Copenhagen's Museum of Decorative Art has begun annual fall exhibitions of new furniture, reprising the traditional Cabinetmaker's Guild exhibitions. In 2002 an international traveling show opened to celebrate the one-hundredth anniversary of Danish architect Arne Jacobsen's birth. And increasingly, London's Design Museum and other prestigious venues have given prominent

1-058

1-059

1-060 1-061

exposure to new design emerging from these resurgent sources.

Newly aware of the importance of design to their several images and states of economic well-being, the Nordic countries, individually and collectively, have begun again to focus on supporting it in order to compete in the international marketplace. Design has become an issue of strategic importance to the Nordic economies, and agendas for design policy are being developed at the highest levels of government. Governmental and industry-supported organizations are initiating new promotional activities, and specialized museums in each country continue to draw attention to developments in design and the decorative arts.

As a new century approached, world-class architectural landmarks have drawn attention to several Scandinavian cities, including Helsinki's Kiasma art museum (designed by an American, Steven Holl), Copenhagen's new library and opera house, and the suspension bridge linking Malmö and Copenhagen. Projects in other countries have brought recognition to Nordic architectural firms such as Norway's Snøhetta (the Alexandria Library in Egypt and a new cultural center building at the World Trade Center site in New York City), and Sweden's Claesson Koivisto Rune (the Ambassador's Residence in Berlin).

In 2003 an exhibition titled Scandinavian Design: Beyond the Myth, marked a joint effort by the five Nordic nations to re-examine the issue

1-060
Two-Faced Chair, Hannu Kähönen, 2006
Producer: Martela

1-061
Clothes Tree, Cecelia Manz, 2000
Producer: PP Møbler
Not in current production

1-062
Space Bench, Flemming Busk+
Stephan B. Hertzog, 2003
Producer: Magnus Olesen
(see also page 206)

1-063
Eshu Sofa, Roger Sveian, 2002
Producer: Mokasser (formerly Leads)
(see also page 178)

1-064
Ugo Sofa, Norway Says, 2003
Producer: LK Hjelle
(see also page 168)

1-062

1-063

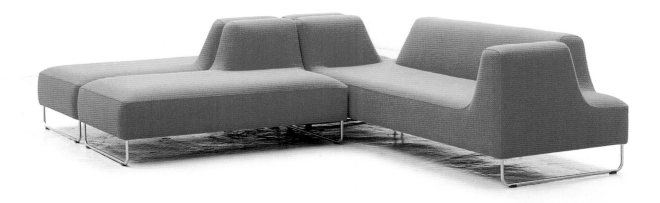

1-064

of national identity, the origins and development of the "Scandinavian design" aesthetic, and the new directions of Nordic design. Accompanied by a scholarly publication of the same name, edited by Widar Halén and Kerstin Wickman in several languages, the exhibition opened in Berlin and traveled through Continental Europe and Scandinavia for the next two years.

In a noteworthy sign of this new awareness, Sweden, Norway, Finland,

and Denmark implemented independent programs to promote 2005 as a "Year of Design." Incorporating competitions, exhibitions, public forums, publications, and a variety of special events, these programs had three critical objectives: to increase public awareness of the importance of design in all areas of everyday life; to encourage producers in various fields to make greater use of designers and design; and to generate international interest in the design output of the individual countries.

A joint world congress of design, called ERA05, was staged in the same year in preliminary venues in Helsinki, Oslo, and Göteborg, with a concluding conference in Copenhagen, where scholars, historians, designers, and industry representatives honored design as contributing to the improvement of life and discussed the long-term role of design in society. This was certainly a broader view of design than had ever before been taken.

Buoyed by the exploding interest in mid-twentieth-century design, classic Scandinavian furniture has found a second life through vintage-furniture dealers and major auction houses, reflecting renewed interest in both old and new designs from these countries. Many classic designs have been returned to production, new retailers specializing in Scandinavian design have opened, and importers

1-065
Friday Sofa, Love Arbén, 2001
Producer: Lammhults

1-066
Armchair, Hans J. Wegner, 1960
(produced 2006)
Producer: Carl Hansen

1-067
Pisa, Pentti Hakala, 2006
Producer: Mobel

1-068
Branch Table, Front Design, 2004
Producer: Front Design
(Photo: Anna Løonnerstam)

1-069
Waves, Anne-Mette Jensen and Marten
Ernst, 1994
Producer: Erik Jørgensen

1-068

1-069

have again begun aggressively to market Scandinavian designs. There is,
however, a notable difference from the mid-century Scandinavian design
phenomenon: the furniture is not necessarily linked to national identity
but is promoted only on the basis of its visual appeal.

The resurgence of creative energy on the part of the current generation of designers has produced innovative furniture—first in Sweden and
Finland, and then in Denmark, Norway, and Iceland—that meets the
rigorous standards of today's sophisticated consumers in a highly compet-

itive market. Good design, though not defined by geography, is informed by the cultural heritage of its makers. Furniture from Denmark, Finland, Iceland, Norway, and Sweden today ranges from classic modern to eccentric avant-garde. It eschews ethnicity in either aesthetics or materials, but continues to express the integrity and humanity of the countries in which it was conceived. In the future, Nordic design may be as much influenced by external factors as it is an influence on them, but it will nevertheless remain a creative source to be reckoned with.

PART II

Contemporary Scandinavian Furniture
A Selective Sourcebook

See page 242

NOTE: Except where otherwise indicated, all items shown were in production at time of writing. However, current status should be confirmed with the individual producer. Materials and finishes may also be subject to change.

Dimensions, converted from metric to imperial measurements or vice-versa, are necessarily approximate. Where measurements or design dates are not given, that information was not provided.

DINING &
OCCASIONAL
CHAIRS

2-001

2-002

2-003

Previous page
2-001
#45 Armchair
Design: Finn Juhl, 1945
Fabric or leather upholstery, teak, pal-
isander, or mahogany frame.
H 27½", W 30¼", D 32½"
(69 x 78 x 82.3 cm)
Producer: Hansen & Sorensen

This page
2-002
#1165
Design: Josef Frank, 1947
Mahogany frame, rattan back, or horsehair
with polyester and synthetic batting.
H 32¾", W 18½", D 22½" (83 x 47 x 57 cm)
Producer: Svenskt Tenn

2-003
Mikado
Design: Foersom & Hiort-Lorenzen
Solid beech or beech and walnut, lac-
quered or bleached, solid walnut spindles
and legs; available with flax or leather
cushion, with or without arms.
With arms: H 35½", W 22¾", D 22"
(90 x 58 x 56 cm)
Armless: H 33¾", W 17¼", D 19¾"
(86 x 44 x 50 cm)
Producer: Fredericia

2-004
#406
Design: Alvar Aalto, 1938–39
Laminated bentwood natural lacquered
birch frame, linen webbing
upholstery, quilted canvas or leather, with
leather belts.
H 28½", W 23½", D 28½" (72 x 60 x 72 cm)
Producer: Artek

2-005
#611
Design: Alvar Aalto, 1929–30
Natural lacquer, stained white, gray, or
black frame; linen webbing or fabric
upholstery; stackable.
H 31½", W 19⅛", D 19¼"
(80 x 48.5 x 49 cm)
Producer: Artek

2-004

2-005

2-008

2-006

2-007

2-006
Series 7, #3107
Design: Arne Jacobsen, 1955
Laminated wood shell, chrome-plated or
satin-polished metal base; with or without
arms, with casters or pedestal base; choice
of 20-plus colors and finishes.
H 30¾", W 19¾", D 20½"
(78 x 50 x 52 cm)
Producer: Fritz Hansen

2-007
#3101 Ant
Design: Arne Jacobsen, 1952
Laminated wood shell, polished metal
base.
H 30¼", W 19", D 19" (77 x 48 x 48 cm)
Producer: Fritz Hansen

2-008
PK-9
Design: Poul Kjærholm, 1960
Leather over pressure-molded fiber-rein-
forced polyester shell, satin-brushed stain-
less steel base.
H 29½", W 22½", D 24" (76 x 56 x 60 cm)
Producer: Fritz Hansen

2-009

2-010

2-009
Gastis # 6123
Design: Åke Axelsson
Natural beech or birch veneer, uphol-
stered seat.
H 32", W 19", D 20½" (81 x 48 x 52.5 cm)
Producer: Gärsnäs

2-010
#4322 Vaxholmaren
Design: Åke Axelsson
Solid beech, loose upholstered
seat pad.
 H 30½", W 21¾", D 22½"
(77.5 x 55 x 57 cm)
Producer: Gärsnäs

2-011
PP 911, Slow Chair
Design: Søren Ulrik Petersen, 2000
Natural ash.
H 26½", W 25", D 25¾"
(67.5 x 63.5 x 65 cm)
Producer: PP Møbler

2-011

2-012

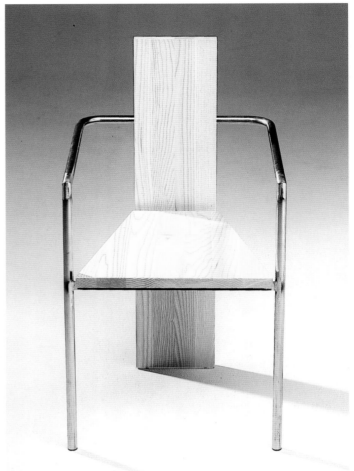

2-013

2-014

2-012
Gute
Design: Mattias Ljunggren, 1999
Beech, natural or stained in standard colors; also available as arm-chair with leather-wrapped arms, leather seat.
H 30¾ ", W 24½", D 22" (78.5 x 62 x 56 cm)
Producer: Källemo

2-013
Concrete
Design: Jonas Bohlin, 1980
Solid ash, natural or stained in standard colors; matte or black steel frame.
H 34¼", W 19¼ ", D 20¾" (87 x 49 x 53 cm)
Producer: Källemo

2-014
Clash
Design: Samuli Naamanka, 2003
Form-pressed birch, beech, oak, walnut, or technical wenge seat and back, matte or gray chrome-plated steel base. Also available uphol-stered, with chrome arms.
H 32", W 19¼", D 20½" (81 x 49 x 52 cm)
Producer: Korhonen division, Martela

2-015

2-016

2-015
GA-1
Design: Erik Gunnar Asplund, 1930
Chrome-plated steel frame, bentwood back; seat frame of wood
with webbing, foam, leather.
H 30¾, W 24½", D 22" (78 x 62 x 56 cm)
Producer: Källemo

2-016
Pampas
Design: Komplot Design, 2004
Natural, black, green, or brown leather, chrome-plated steel frame.
H 32", W 23", D 20" (82 x 58 x 53 cm)
Producer: Källemo

2-017
#EJ 96, Apollo
Design: Johannes Foersom and Peter Hiort-Lorenzen, 2000
Molded polyurethane foam seat and back, fixed covers, stainless
steel swivel base with memory return.
H 30", W 31½", D 27" (76 x 80 x 69 cm)
Producer: Erik Jørgensen

2-017

2-018   2-019   2-020

2-018
PP 501 Round Chair ("The Chair")
Design: Hans J. Wegner, 1949
Oak, ash, mahogany, cherry, or teak frame,
woven cane, leather, or fabric seat.
H 30", W 24¾", D 20½" (76 x 63 x 52 cm)
Producer: PP Møbler

2-019
PP 505, The Cow Horn Chair
Design: Hans J. Wegner, 1952
Oak, ash, maple, mahogany, or cherry.
H 29¼", W 23¼", D 17¾" (74 x 59 x 45 cm)
Producer: PP Møbler

2-020
China Chair
Design: Hans J. Wegner, 1944
Lacquered mahogany or cherry, leather
cushion.
H 32¼", W 21¾", D 21¾" (82 x 55 x 55 cm)
Produceer: PP Møbler

2-021
China Chair
Design: Hans J. Wegner, 1943
Mahogany or cherry frame, buttoned
leather cushion.
H 32¼", W 21¾", D 21¾" (82 x 55 x 55 cm)
Producer: Fritz Hansen

2-021

2-022
T-stol
Design: Ole Wanscher, 1958
Rosewood frame, fabric or leather seat.
Producer: P. J. Furniture

2-023
Pastillo
Design: Ulla Christiansson, 2004
Steel frame, fabric seat pads.
H 32", W 17¾", D 18½" (81 x 45 x 47 cm)
Producer: Karl Andersson

2-024
Trippo
Design: Ulla Christiansson, 2000
Oak back, fabric padded seat, steel legs.
H 29¼", W 18½", D 17" (74 x 47 x 43 cm)
Producer: Karl Andersson

2-022

2-023

2-024

2-025

2-025
Innovation C
Design: Fredrik Mattson, 2002
Fabric over molded polyurethane, steel,
and wood frame, stainless steel base;
auto-return available.
H 29", W 27", D 25" (74 x 69 x 64 cm)
Producer: Blå Station

2-026
Dome
Design: Asko Lax, 1998
Molded plywood, natural lacquer or
stained, tapered steel tubular legs;
optional upholstered seat; available with-
out arms; stackable.
H 31", W 18", D 18" (79 x 46 x 46 cm)
Producer: Piiroinen

2-026

2-027

2-027
#9870 Chair
Design: Bernt, 1998
Beech, maple, or ash, chrome-plated or
powder-lacquered metal frame.
H 33", W 20¾ ", D 21¼" (84 x 53 x 54 cm)
Producer: Getama
(Photo: Erik Brahl)

2-028
Bollo
Design: Kaarle Holmberg, 2003
Pressed veneer, metal frame, natural,
stained beech, or upholstered seat.
H 33½ ", W 22½", D 32½"
(85 x 60 x 57 cm)
Producer: Lepo Product

2-029
CH 24
Design: Hans J. Wegner, 1949
Maple, ash, beech, oak, or cherry.
H 29½", W 21¾", D 20" (75 x 55 x 51 cm)
Producer: Carl Hansen
(Photo: Søren Larson)

2-030
#4594 Light & Easy
Design: Åke Axelsson
Natural ash or beech, with veneer or
upholstered seat.
H 32¼", W 20½", D 19¾ (82 x 52 x 50)
Producer: Gärsnäs

2-028

2-029

2-030

2-031

2-031
Gemini
Design: Ola Rune, 2004
Fabric or leather upholstery, birch veneer frame, steel frame with chrome or gray lacquer finish; also available as two-seat sofa.
H 30¼", W 26", D 24¼" (77 x 66 x 62 cm)
Producer: Swedese

2-032
#4570 Big Hug
Design: Anna von Schewen, 2002
Solid bentwood seat, open sides or upholstered inserts, fabric or leather upholstery optional, steel tubing frame.
H 29", W 22", D 20" (74 x 56 x 51 cm)
Producer: Gärsnäs

2-033
Kilta
Design: Olli Mannermaa, 1955, reissued 2001
Patented construction, one-piece molded polyurethane frame, fully upholstered, chrome-plated or gray-painted steel base; available without armrests, with four-leg base.
H 30", W 25", D 25" (76 x 64 x 64 cm)
Producer: Martela

2-032

2-033

2-034

2-034
Triennale Chair
Design: Antti Nurmesniemi, 1960
Seat and back upholstered with nappa
leather, steel-plated frame.
H 31½", W 20½", D 20½"
(80 x 52 x 52 cm)
Producer: Piiroinen

2-035
Mono Light
Design: Ola Rune, 2004
Seat and back upholstered in fabric or
leather; or natural, stained, or lacquered
birch, chrome-plated or silver-
lacquered metal runners; available with
arms. Companion barstool seat and back
cold foam with Pullmaflex spring system.
Chair: H 28", W 25", D 23½"
(71 x 64 x 60 cm)
Barstool: H 38", W 22½" (97, 57 cm)
Producer: Offecct
(Photo: Peter Fotograf)

2-035

2-036

2-036
Tina
Design: Yrjö Wiherheimo and Pekka Kojo, 1984
Laminated natural or stained birch, natural beech, or oak seat and back, wood arms; powder-coated, painted black, gray, white, or aluminum, or chrome-plated tubular steel frame and legs.
H 34½", W 24", D 22" (88 x 61 x 56 cm)
Producer: Vivero

2-037
Bird
Design: Yrjö Wiherheimo and Pekka Kojo, 1993
Laminated plywood in several finishes; steel or wood base.
H 29½", W 25½", D 25" (75 x 65 x 64 cm)
Producer: Vivero

2-038
Papi
Design: Yrjö Wiherheimo and Pekka Kojo, 1983
Translucent white or gunmetal gray molded fiberglass seat and back, powder-painted or chrome-plated tubular steel base.
H 31½", W 29", D 24¼" (80 x 74 x 61.5 cm)
Producer: Vivero

2-038

2-037

2-039

2-040

2-039
Chair #71
Design: N. O. Møller, 1950s
Teak
H 31", W 19¼", D 20" (79 x 49 x 51 cm)
Producer: J. L. Møller

2-040
Chairs #78 and #62
Design: N. O. Møller, 1954
Oak, cherry, maple, rosewood, or teak, upholstered seat.
#78: H 31½", W 19", D 20½" (80 x 48 x 52 cm);
 #62: H 31", W 22", D 21¾" (79 x 56 x 55 cm)
Producer: J. L. Møllers

2-041
Bessi
Design: Erla Sølveig Óskarsdóttir, 2001
Fully upholstered seat and back, stainless steel frame.
H 33", W 15", D 22" (80 x 38 x 56 cm)
Producer: Hansen & Sorensen

2-041

2-043

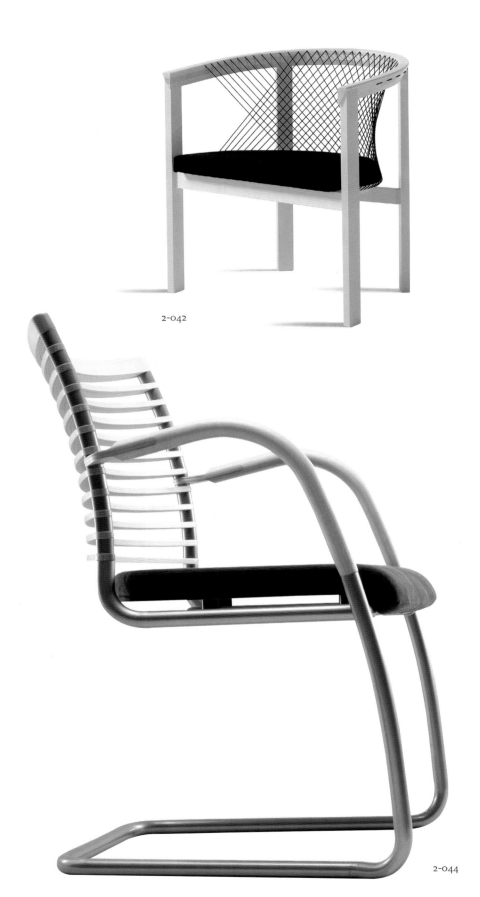

2-042

2-044

2-042
NJH Easy Chair
Design: Niels Jørgen Haugesen
Birch, rope; available as side chair
Producer: Axelsen

2-043
Iris
Design: Bob van den Berghe, 1982
Beech, oak, cherry, or walnut, upholstered
seat; available without arms.
H 44", W 27½" (armless 20½"), D 19¾"
(112 x 70 [armless 52] x 50 cm)
Producer: Tranekaer

2-044
Zebra II
Design: Johnny Sørensen, 2001
Laminated beech, maple, or cherry, uphol-
stered seat, wood arms; cantilevered steel
base or stackable with legs.
H 25", W 21½", D 21½" (63.5 x 55 x 55 cm)
Producer: Magnus Olesen

2-045

2-046

2-045
#4380 Tati
Design: Ralf Lindberg
Birch, beech, or oak veneer seat and back, wood frame.
H 31½", W 19¼", D 16¼" (80 x 49 x 41 cm)
Producer: Gärsnäs

2-046
Rex
Design: Christina Strand, 2002
Lacquered birch and walnut on metal base. Upholstery available.
Producer: Fredericia

2-047
Aron
Design: Love Arbén, 1989
Leather or fabric upholstery, chrome-plated or powder-coated steel frame.
H 29", W 21", D 20" (74 x 54 x 51 cm)
Producer: Lammhults

2-047

2-048

2-048
Lotus
Design: Flemming Busk + Stephan B. Hertzog
Fabric-upholstered shell, stainless metal frame.
H 29½", W 28½", D 25½" (75 x 72 x 65 cm)
Producer: Globe

Opposite
2-049
Voxia Collection-Oto
Design: Peter Karpf 1982, produced 2002
Natural, stained, or lacquered beech; one-piece construction without screws or joints.
H 28", W 30¾", D 24" (71 x 78 x 61 cm)
Producer: Iform

2-050
Oto
Design: Peter Karpf, 1982, introduced 2002
Laminated beech, birch, or oak, with flexible back, available with upholstered seat or upholstered seat and back, also with low arm.
H 31¼", W 20", D 22¼" (79 x 51 x 56 cm)
Producer: Kinnarps

2-051
Visa
Design: Pentti Hakala, 1991–2
Molded birch plywood shell, natural or stained, tubular steel frame; may be upholstered in fabric or leather.
H 32¼", W 24½", D 23¼" (82 x 62 x 59 cm)
Producer: Mobel

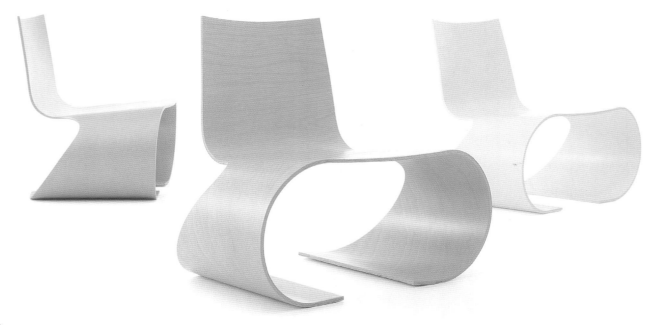

2-049

2-050

2-051

2-052

2-052
Faaborgstöl
Design: Kaare Klint, 1914
Mahogany or cherry frame, cane back,
oxhide seat.
H 28¾", W 25½", D 27½" (73 x 64 x 70 cm)
Producer: Rud. Rasmussen

2-053
Safari Chair
Design: Kaare Klint, 1933
Mahogany or cherry, leather or canvas seat
and back.
H 32", W 22¾", D 22¾" (81 x 58 x 58 cm)
Producer: Rud. Rasmussen

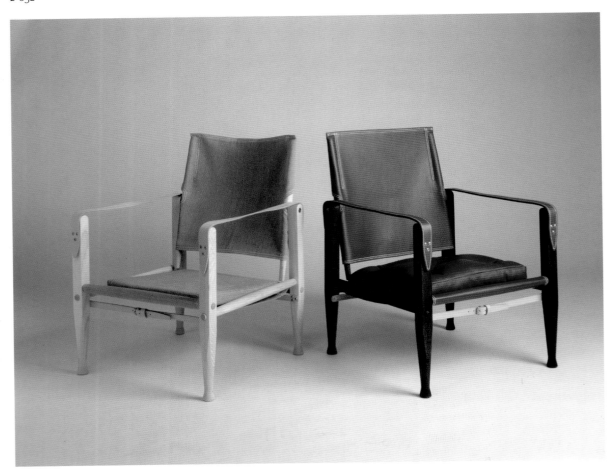

2-053

2-054
Pimpim
Design: John Kandell
Lacquered birch in red or green.
H 33½", W 19¾", D 19"
(85 x 50 x 48 cm)
Producer: Källemo

2-055
Graf
Design: KODE, 2002
Highback chair, laminated birch,
steel legs; available with low back,
with or without upholstery, with
steel swivel base, and barstool height.
Producer: EFG

2-056
Cuba
Design: Alexander Lervik
Fabric upholstery over foam, chrome-
plated steel base.
Producer: Johanson Design

2-054

2-055

2-056

LOUNGE
CHAIRS

Previous page
2-057
Attitude
Design: Morten Voss, 2004
Lounge series, upholstered in fabric or leather over
molded foam core, powder-coated steel base in matte or
textured silver-gray finish. Return swivel mechanism.
Coordinating table available.
H 27½", L 26¾", D 29¾" (70 x 68 x 76 cm)
Producer: Fritz Hansen

2-058
PK-20
Design: Poul Kjærholm, 1956
Leather over tubular steel frame.
H 33 or 31½", W 31½", D 26¾ or 30"
(84 or 80 x 80 x 80 x 68 or 76 cm)
Producer: Fritz Hansen

Opposite
2-059
PK-22
Design: Poul Kjærholm, 1956
Wicker over tubular steel frame; also avail-
able in leather.
H 28", W 24¾", D 24¾" (71 x 63 x 63)
Producer: Fritz Hansen

2-060
PK-25
Design: Poul Kjærholm, 1951
Flag halyard rope seat and back, tubular
steel frame.
H 29½", W 27¼", D 28¾" (75 x 69 x 73 cm)
Producer: Fritz Hansen

2-061
#472 Skaala
Design: Yrjö Kukkapuro, 1980–81
Formed birch plywood seat, back, and
armrests with natural edges, black
laminate facing, chrome-plated steel tubing base. Also available as lounge chair
(left).
H 34½", W 24", D 25¼" (88 x 61 x 64 cm)
Producer: Avarte

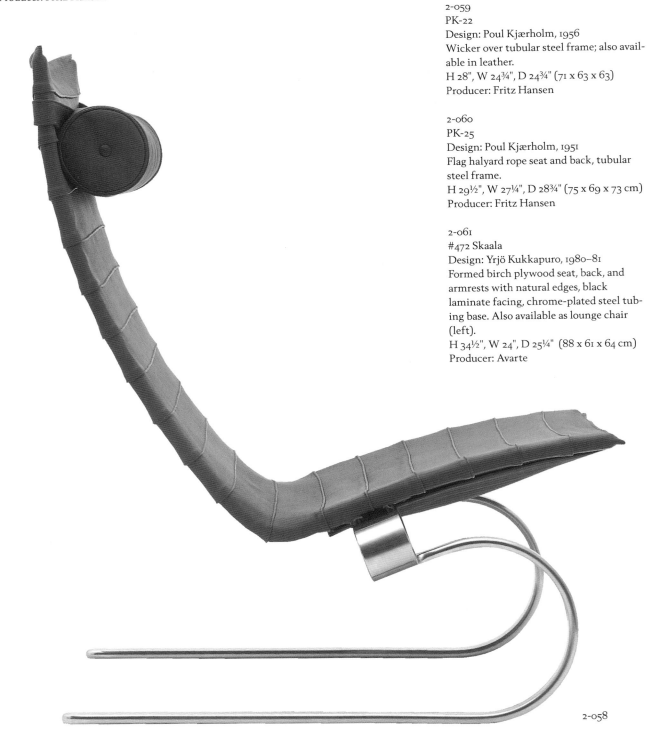

2-058

2-059

2-060

2-061

2-062

2-062
Split #4590
Design: Anna von Schewen, 2003
Easy chair with separate seating elements,
various upholstery options. Beech, oak, or
birch frame.
Producer: Gärsnäs

2-063
KS-172 Jefferson
Design: Alexander Lervik, 2004
Fabric upholstery over polyether foam,
tubular steel frame and legs, casters.
H 32¼", W 26", D 23¼" (82 x 66 x 59 cm)
Producer: Skandiform

2-063

2-064
#3320 Swan
Design: Arne Jacobsen, 1958
Leather or fabric upholstery over molded
polyurethane, cast aluminum swivel base.
H 30¼", W 29¼", D 26¾" (77 x 74 x 68 cm)
Producer: Fritz Hansen

2-065
#3316 Egg with #3127 Ottoman
Design: Arne Jacobsen, 1958
Fabric or leather over molded polyure-
thane, cast aluminum swivel base.
H 42¼", W 33¾", D 31 or 37½"
(107 x 86 x 79 or 95 cm)
Ottoman: H 14½", W 22" (37 x 56 cm)
Producer: Fritz Hansen

2-064

2-065

2-066
Planet
Design: Sven Ivar Dysthe, 1965
Stretchable fabric upholstery, chrome
base with solid beech inserts.
Producer: Fora Form

2-067
Loop
Design: Johan Verde, 2002
Stretch fabric, metal frame, polished
aluminum base with rollers.
Producer: Foraform

2-066

2-067

2-068
Orbit
Design: Eero Koivisto, 2001
Fabric or leather upholstery over molded cold-foam, laminated wood frame, chrome-plated or lacquered metal legs.
H 31½", W 39¼", D 29" (80 x 100 x 74 cm)
Producer: Offecct
(Photo: Peter Fotograf)

2-069
Easy Chair
Design: Knud Færch, 1995
Upholstery fabric over cold-foam and Hollofill on wood framework, matte chrome-plated steel frame; available with swivel base.
H 37½ or 32¾", W 29½", D 26¾"
(95 or 83 x 75 x 68 cm)
Producer: Källemo

2-068

2-069

2-070
#EJ 5 Corona
Design: Poul M. Volther, 1964
Molded polyurethane foam, fixed fabric or
leather upholstery, matte chrome-plated
steel frame and legs.
H 38¼", W 34¾", D 32¼" (97 x 88 x 82 cm)
Producer: Erik Jørgensen

2-070b

2-070a

2-071

Tinto Center
Design: Claesson Koivisto Rune, 2003
Fabric or leather upholstery over molded
cold-foam, chrome-plated or silver-
lacquered metal foot; available with
tubular metal legs.
H 26¾", W 30", D 18½" (68 x 76 x 47 cm)
Producer: Offecct (Photo: Peter Fotograf)

2-072

#EJ 100 Oxchair
Design: Hans J. Wegner, 1960
Leather upholstery over molded polyure-
thane foam, matte chrome-plated steel
legs; companion ottoman.
H 35½", W 39", D 39" (90 x 99 x 99)
Producer: Erik Jørgensen

2-071

2-072

2-073

2-073
Theselius Easy Chair
Design: Mats Theselius, 1990
Leather or suede over foam seat and back,
polished or matte aluminum wood frame,
cast aluminum legs.
H 27½", W 2½", D 24½" (70 x 60 x 62 cm)
Producer: Källemo

2-074
Ambassad
Design: Mats Theselius, 1999
Riveted prime natural, black, green, or
brown leather, cold-foam seat, matte
chrome- or copper-plated steel frame.
H 29½", W 21¼", D 21" (75 x 54 x 53 cm)
Producer: Källemo

2-074

2-075
PP 19 Papa Bear
Design: Hans J. Wegner, 1954
Upholstery over wood frame, teak arm caps and legs;
companion footstool available.
H 39¾", W 35½", D 37½" (102 x 90 x 95 cm)
Producer: PP Møbler

2-076
PP 225 Flag Halyard Chair
Design: Hans J. Wegner, 1950
Sheepskin over flag halyard rope seat and back,
steel frame, upholstered head pillow.
H 31", D 40", W 45" (80 x 102 x 115 cm)
Producer: PP Møbler

2-075

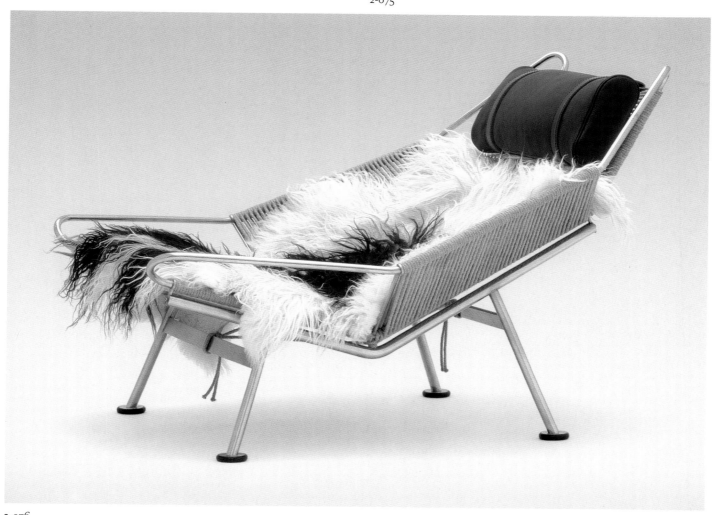

2-076

2-077

2-077
PP 124 Rocking Chair
Design: Hans J. Wegner, 1988
Ash, plaited flag halyard rope, leather
seat cushion.
H 42½", W 29½", D 34¾" (108 x 75 x 88 cm)
Producer: PP Møbler

2-078
#J16 Rocking Chair
Design: Hans J. Wegner, 1944
Beech or oak; available untreated, bleached, natural,
or black-lacquered.
H 42¼", W 24¾", D 36½" (107 x 63 x 93 cm)
Producer: Fredericia

2-078

2-079
Scandia Nett Lounge Chair
Design: Hans Brattrud, 1957
Laminated walnut or other woods,
chrome-plated steel legs; available with
high back, with swivel-base,
or stackable.
H 28", W 25", D 29" (71 x 63.5 x 74 cm)
Producer: Fjord Fiesta
(Photo: Hugo Opdal)

2-080
P 512 Folding Chair
Design: Hans J. Wegner, 1949
Ash or beech, woven cane; can hang on
wall when closed.
H 30", W 24", D 29" (77 x 61 x 75 cm)
Producer: PP Møbler

2-079

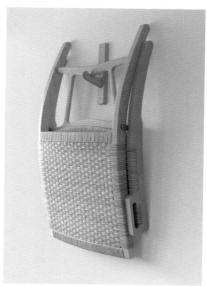

2-080a

2-080b

2-081
Toad Lounge Chair
Design: Ruud Ekstrand, 2002
Fabric over deep-stitched cushion with fiberfill, white or matte chrome-plated tubular steel base.
H 33", W 35½", D 41" (84 x 90 x 104 cm)
Producer: David Design

2-082
Nietos
Design: Mikko Paakkanen, 2002
Fabric cushioning over formed bleached birch plywood shell, tubular metal base.
H 32", W 39¾", D 28¼"
(81.5 x 101 x 71.5 cm)
Producer: Avarte

2-081

2-082

2-083
Hole
Design: Jouni Kaili, 2001
Fabric or leather upholstery over foam, steel frame.
H 27¼", W 35¾", D 28" (69 x 91 x 71 cm)
Producer: Formverk

2-083

2-084
Spanish Chair
Design: Børge Mogensen, 1958
Natural or black leather seat and back,
laquered or natural finish oak frame.
H 26¾", W 32¾", D 24½" (68 x 83 x 62 cm)
Producer: Fredericia

2-085
PJ 149 Colonial Chair
Design: Ole Wanscher, 1947
Rosewood, woven cane, loose cushions.
H 26", W 26½", D 34" (66 x 67 x 86 cm)
Producer: P. J. Furniture

2-086
Kajenne
Design: Christina Fürst, 2002
Oak with leather seat pads.
H 29½", W 22¾", D 28¼" (75 x 58 x 72 cm)
Producer: Karl Andersson

2-084

2-085

2-086

2-087

2-087
Karuselli
Design: Yrjö Kukkapuro, 1964
Leather upholstery over molded fiberglass seat shell, swivel base.
H 36¼", W 31½", D 38½" (92 x 80 x 97.5 cm)
Producer: Avarte

2-088
David
Design: Flemming Busk + Stephan B. Hertzog
Modern rocker, upholstered shell with removable cover over poly-ether foam, matte satin chrome-plated metal frame.
H 28¾", W 35½", D 30¾" (73 x 90 x 78 cm)
Producer: Softline

2-089
Remmi
Design: Yrjö Kukkapuro, 1970–72
Leather upholstery over chrome-plated tubular steel frame; companion ottoman.
H 33½", W 28", D 36" (85.5 x 71 x 91.5 cm)
Producer: Avarte

2-088

2-089

2-090a

2-090
Scimitar
Design: Preben Fabricius and Jørgen
Kastholm, 1984 (reintroduced 2006)
Leather over shell, stainless steel frame
and base.
H 26", W 32¾", D 27¼" (66 x 83 x 69.5 cm)
Producer: Bo-Ex

2-091
Snooze
Design: Stefan Borselius and Fredrik
Mattson, 2004
Fabric or leather over hot-molded foam,
chrome-plated tubular steel base.
H 25", W 25½", D 20" (63.5 x 65 x 51 cm)
Producer: Blå Station

2-090b

2-091

2-092

2-092
#460 Butterfly Easy Chair
Design: Hans J. Wegner, 1977
Beech, oak, or maple, fabric or leather upholstery.
H 26¾", W 25¼", D 28" (68 x 64 x 71 cm)
Producer: Getama (Photo: Erik Brahl)

2-093
290A High Back Easy Chair
Design: Hans J. Wegner, 1953
Beech or oak, fabric or leather upholstered cushions.
H 38½", W 30", D 33" (98 x 76 x 84 cm)
Producer: Getama (Photo: Erik Brahl)

2-093

2-094

2-095

2-096

2-094
CH 25
Design: Hans J. Wegner, 1950
Oak frame, rope seat and back.
H 28¾", W 28", D 28¾" (73 x 71 x 73 cm)
Producer: Carl Hansen
(Photo: Søren Larson)

2-095
CH 44
Design: Hans J. Wegner, 1965
Ash, beech, oak, or cherry back
and frame, woven seat; optional
seat and back cushions.
H 31½", 25¼", D 26"
(80 x 64 x 66 cm)
Producer: Carl Hansen

2-096
CH 07 Three-legged Shell
Design: Hans J. Wegner, 1963
Laminated maple, oak, or walnut,
fabric or leather upholstery.
H 29¼", W 36¼", D 32¾"
(74 x 92 x 83 cm)
Producer: Carl Hansen
(Photo: Søren Larson)

2-097
Paris Chair
Design: Arne Jacobsen, 1925
Natural rattan cane.
H 32", W 25½", D 45¼" (81 x 65 x 115 cm)
Producer: The Canemaker, division of
JV Holding

2-097

2-098
Matto
Design: Kaarle Holmberg, 2003
Laminated veneer in natural or stained
birch, pressed to bend in three directions,
metal legs; available upholstered.
Producer: Lepo Product

2-099
AJ 235
Design: Arne Jacobsen, 1930
Natural rattan cane
H 32", W 25", D 45¼" (81 x 63.5 x 115)
Producer: The Canemaker, division of
JV Holding

2-098

2-099

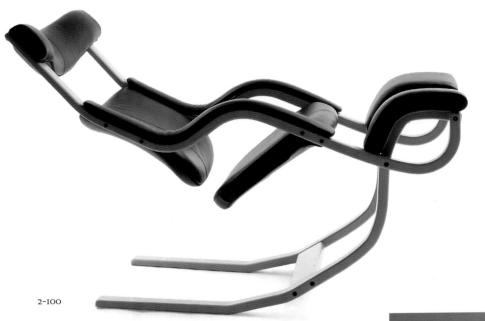

2-100

2-101

2-102

2-100
Gravity
Design: Peter Opsvik, 1982
Beech, cherry, rosewood, mocha brown,
or black wood, fabric or leather uphol-
stery. Rocking variation of Balans seating
collection.
Producer: Varier

2-101
Rock n' Roll
Design: Sigurdur Gústafsson, 1998
Polished sheet and tubular stainless steel.
H 27", W 22", D 36½" (69 x 56 x 93 cm)
Producer: Källemo

2-102
Peel Adjustable Lounge Chair
Design: Olav Eldøy, Johan Verde, 2001
Patented design adjusts with weight shift
to rock, recline, or swivel. Laminated
beech in choice of finishes or fabric over
foam; left and right versions.
H 44–47¼", W 32¼", D 17¾"
(112–120 x 82 x 45 cm)
Producer: Variér

2-103
People
Design: Thomas Bernstrand,
2005
Leather upholstery over high-
resilience foam, fiberglass-
supported polyester frame, flexible extension leg rest, tubular
steel swivel base.
H 42½", W 26", L 34–47¼"
(108 x 66 x 86–120 cm)
Producer: Swedese

2-104
Lamino
Design: Yngve Ekström, 2003
Beech, oak, cherry, oak/teak,
or walnut, fabric or leather
upholstery; companion footstool. Available in ¾-size child's
version.
H 39¾", W 27½", D 30¾"
(101 x 70 x 78 cm)
Producer: Swedese

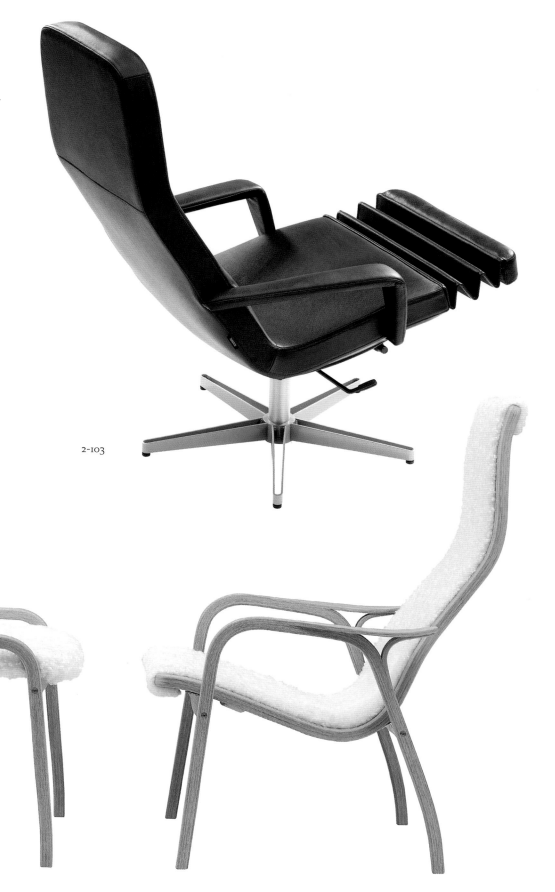

2-103

2-104

2-105

2-106

2-107

2-105
Arcus
Design: Timo Ripatti, 2000
Fabric upholstery over foam on pressed
plywood shell, or with seat and back in
natural or stained birch, natural beech, or
oak, on tubular steel frame.
H 30", W 34½", D 28¾" (76 x 87 x 73 cm)
Producer: Vivero

2-106
Soft
Design: Kai Korhonen, 2005
High-back easy chair, fabric over polyure-
thane foam, steel frame; available with low
back and as sofa.
H 78¾", W 55", D 60" (200 x 140 x 152 cm)
Producer: Vivero

2-107
PP 130 Hoop Chair
Design: Hans J. Wegner 1965 (produced
1986)
Ash, flag halyard rope, fabric cushions.
H 38¼", W 44", D 37" (97 x 112 x 94 cm)
Producer: PP Møbler

2-108

2-109

2-108
Jive
Design: Anders Nørgaard
Upholstered shells with foam fill, steel base.
H 31", W 78", D 31" (79 x 198 x 79 cm)
Producer: Globe

2-109
Mondial
Design: Nanna Ditzel, 2000
Fabric or leather upholstery, wood frame.
H 29¼", W 30¾ or 32¾", D 29¼"
(74 x 78 or 83 x 74)
Producer: Getama (Photo: Erik Brahl)

2-110
Stingray Rocking Chair
Design: Thomas Pedersen
Vacuum-formed black or
white plastic shell, steel frame.
Producer: Fredericia

2-110

2-III

2-II3

2-II2

2-III
Zip
Design: Tom Stepp
Natural cotton or microfiber zip-off cov-
ers or fixed leather covers, chrome-steel
memory-return swivel base.
H 28½", W 30¼", D 19¾" (72 x 77 x 50 cm)
Producer: Stouby

2-II2
#9830 Jass
Design: Tom Stepp, 2005
Fabric or leather upholstery; brushed
aluminum pedestal base, or tubular metal
legs; coordinating sofa available.
H 42½", W 29¼", D 36" (108 x 74 x 91 cm)
Producer: Stouby

2-II3
Tuesday
Design: Love Arbén, 2002
Fabric over cold-pressed polyether foam,
wood frame, casters.
H 29½", W 22", D 21" (75 x 56 x 53 cm)
Producer: Lammhults

2-114
Mademoiselle
Design: Ilmari Tapiovaara, 1956
Solid birch seat, back, and base.
H 36½", W 21½", D 25¾"
(92.5 x 54.5 x 65.5 cm)
Producer: Aero

2-115
Select
Design: Harri Korhonen, 2001
Upholstered easy chair, with square
or X-shape pedestal base, both with
memory-return swivel, or on steel legs.
Also available with arms.
H 31¼", W 23¼", D 26¾" (79 x 59 x 68 cm)
Producer: Inno

2-114

2-115

2-116
Prime Time
Design: Tom Stepp
Birch, beech, walnut, or bleached oak
steam-bent shell, loose reversible
cushions.
H 29½", W 22½", D 21¼" (75 x 57 x 54 cm)
Producer: Fredericia

2-116

2-117
Carat
Design: Christina and Lars Andersson, 2001
Fabric over foam on metal base; available as
armchair or two-seat sofa.
Producer: EFG

2-118
Chieftain Chair
Design: Finn Juhl, 1949
Walnut, leather upholstery.
H 37½", W 41", D 36½" (95 x 104 x 93 cm)
Producer: Hansen & Sorensen

2-119
Domus
Design: Ilmari Tapiovaara, 1946
Laminated natural birch.
H 31", W 22", D 21¼" (79 x 56 x 54 cm)
Producer: Aero

2-120
Neptunus I, # 6202
Design: Åke Axelsson
Solid natural birch or oak frame,
upholstered seat and back.
Producer: Gärsnäs

2-118

2-119

2-120

2-121

2-121
Open
Design: Eva and Peter Moritz, 2005
Fabric upholstery over high-resilience
foam, laminated wood veneer frame,
aluminum or chrome-plated steel swivel
base; matching stool and companion table
with white laminated or birch top.
Chair: H 32¼", W 21¼", D 26"
(82 x 54 x 66 cm)
Producer: Swedese

2-122
Whole in One™
Design: Nora Furuholmen
and Christian Saethe, 2001
Stretch upholstery over foam on steel
base.
H 34", W 43¾", D 43¾" (86 x 111 x 111 cm)
Producer: Mokasser

2-123
Aurora
Design: Jørn Utzon, 1965
Fabric upholstery over foam, laminated
maple shell, tubular steel frame.
H 30", W 35¾", D 38¾" (76 x 91 x 98 cm)
Producer: Bahnsen/TRIOLINE

2-122

2-123

2-124

2-125

2-126

2-124
Metro
Design: Thomas Sandell, 2004
Fabric or leather upholstery over molded cold-foam with Pullmaflex spring system; chrome-plated or lacquered metal legs.
H 31", W 22", D 18½" (79 x 56 x 47 cm)
Producer: Offecct (Photo: Peter Fotograf)

2-125
Graf
Design: Dan Ihreborn, 1999
Handwoven rope, steel.
H 21", W 23", D 16" (53 x 58 x 41 cm)
Producer: Kallin & Franzén (Move-range)

2-126
PP 550 Peacock Chair
Design: Hans J. Wegner, 1947
Ash or teak, paper-cord seat.
H 42", W 28", D 27" (107 x 71 x 69 cm)
Producer: PP Møbler

2-127
Ekstrem
Design: Terje Ekstrem, 1972 (produced from 1984)
Knit fabric upholstery, six colors, over
polyurethane, metal frame, optional wood feet.
H 31–32¾", W 30", D 29½" (79–83 x 76 x 75 cm)
Producer: Variér

2-128
Pelikan
Design: Finn Juhl, 1940
Handsewn upholstery over foam, frame maple
or other woods.
H 34¾", W 31¼", D 28¾" (88 x 79 x 74 cm)
Producer: Hansen & Sorensen

2-129
Peekaboo
Design: Stefan Borselius, 2005
Formed felt outer shell, Alcantara interior, chromed
tubular steel legs; optional drop-down front hood
with clear plastic front.
H 47¾ W 27½", D 30" (121 x 70 x 76 cm)
Producer: Blå Station

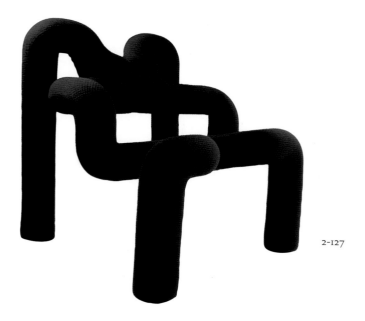

2-127

2-128

2-129

2-130

2-131

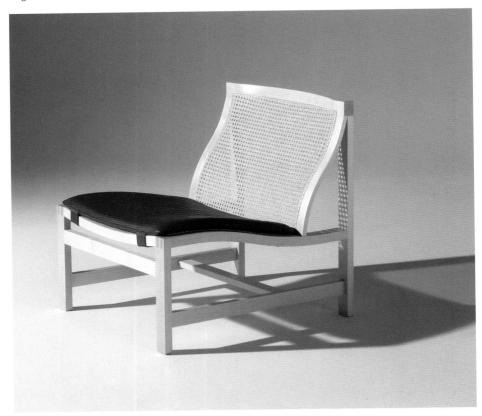

2-132

2-130
Skyseat
Design: Sigurdur Gustafsson, 2000
Aluminum with black, red, green, or blue lacquered MDF, limited edition of 200.
H 30¾", W 31½", D 29½" (78 x 80 x 75 cm)
Producer: Källemo

2-131
Gothem
Design: Kristian Eriksson, 2003
Fabric upholstery over solid wood frame.
H 28¾", W 24¾", D 31½" (73 x 63 x 80 cm)
Producer: G.A.D.

2-132
#7501 King's Chair
Design: Rud Thygesen and Johnny Sørensen, 1969
Maple, mahogany, oak, or cherry with woven cane; leather cushion.
H 28", W 24½", D 28" (71 x 62 x 71 cm)
Producer: Fredericia

2-133
Easy Chair
Design: Nirvan Richter, 1995
Solid beech or ash, natural or oil finish,
or painted in choice of twelve colors.
Fabric, leather, or sheepskin feather-filled
seat cushion, horsehair and wadding over
hemp webbing; optional back cushion.
Coordinated sofa and footstool available.
H 41¾", W 31½", D 29" (106 x 80 x 74 cm)
Producer: Norrgavel

2-134
Classic Seating
Design: Bernt
Mahogany or elm, handwoven cane back
and sides; seat cushions. Available as high-
back chair, armchair, two-seat sofa.
Producer: Søborg

2-133

2-134

2-135

2-135
The Harp
Design: Jørgen Høvelskov, 1963
Natural ash, black-stained ash, cherry, or natural oak, flag halyard
seat and back; frame has single center bolt, folds flat.
H 53", W 42", D 40" (135 x 107 x 102 cm)
Producer: J. Christensens

2-136
Z-Down
Design: Erik Magnussen, 1940
Natural, brown, or black leather, glossy or
matte chrome-plated frame.
H 27½", W 28½", D 22¾" (70 x 72 x 58 cm)
Producer: Engelbrechts

2-137
Select
Design: Roger Persson, 2005
High back and wrap sides, upholstery over
foam, tubular steel frame; available with wood
frame and legs. Companion footstool.
Chair: H 43¾", W 31¼", D 29½"
(111 x 79 x 75 cm)
Footstool: H 18½ or 16½ ", W 19¾", D 16½"
(47 # or 43 x 50 x 43 cm)
Swedese

2-136

2-137

STACKING
CHAIRS

2-139

2-139
KS 200 and KS 210 Ice
Design: Kasper Salto, 2002
Rigid molded synthetic, aluminum;
available in six colors, with or without
arms, also upholstered, for indoor or
outdoor use.
H 31", W 19¾" (with arms 22"), D 19"
(79 x 50 or 56 x 48 cm)
Producer: Fritz Hansen

Previous page

2-138
Trinidad
Design: Nana Ditzel, 1993
Fan-shaped fretwork on back, maple,
cherry, beech, birch, or walnut seat and back with
fan-shape fretwork, tubular steel frame; optional
upholstered seat, armrests. Also available in black or
white lacquer or nine colors, and as barstool.
H 33¼", W 19", D 22" (84 x 48 x 57 cm)
Producer: Fredericia

2-140

2-141

2-140
#6113 Baltic Armchair
Design: Åke Axelsson
Steel tubing frame with clear or alumi-
num-color lacquer, aluminum back and
seat; molded polyurethane armrests;
upholstery.
Producer: Gärsnäs

2-141
Scandia Junior
Design: Hans Brattrud, 1957
Laminated walnut or other wood, steel
tubing base; available in high-back or
swivel versions.
H 32", W 21", D 20" (81 x 53 x 51 cm)
Producer: Fjord Fiesta
(Photo: Hugo Opdal)

2-142
#6110 Anselm Armchair
Design: Åke Axelsson
Natural or stained birch seat, back, and
front legs, natural birch or oak armrests
and rear legs.
Producer: Gärsnäs

2-142

2-143

2-144

2-143
#4359-A Sar
Design: Åke Axelsson
Natural or stained solid beech wood frame.
H 30¾", W 21¼", D 20¾" (78 x 54 x 53 cm)
Producer: Gärsnäs

2-144
Cobra
Design: Mattias Ljunggren, 1990
Natural birch or oak, colored lacquer, white- or black-stained seat and back or upholstered in fabric, leather, or felt, chrome-plated steel frame and legs.
H 35", W 16½", D 20½" (89 x 42 x 52 cm)
Producer: Källemo

2-145
Non
Design: Komplot Design, 2001
Steel frame encased in PUR-rubber with Feathersteel in back, black, gray, red, or green.
H 30¼", W 17¼", D 15¼" (77 x 44 x 39 cm)
Producer: Källemo

2-145

2-146
Profili T
Design: Simo Heikkilä, 2003
Seat and backrest of formed birch ply-
wood faced in melamine laminate, steel
legs.
H 33¾", W 18½", D 20¼" (86 x 47 x 52 cm)
Producer: Avarte

2-147
Viper
Design: Kajsa Nordström and
Henning Eklund
Compression-molded birch, oak, or black
or white melamine seat, solid steel frame.
Producer: Klaessons

2-146

2-147

2-148

2-149

2-150

2-148
Koldinghus Chair
Design: Hans J. Wegner, 1988
Solid beech; available with or without arms;
can be linked with wood rail.
H 32", W 20¼" (with arms 24½"), D 20¼"
(81 x 51 or 62 x 52 cm)
Producer: Getama (Photo: Erik Brahl)

2-149
Vera
Design: Teemu Järvi, 2000
Birch, oak, ash, or leather-upholstered
seat, chrome-steel frame; available in three
heights.
H 30, 26, or 17½", W 16½", D 15¾, 15, or 13¼"
(76, 66, 44.5 x 42 x 40, 38, 33.5 cm)
Producer: HKT Korhonen

2-150
#3800 Zig Armchair
Design: Bernt, 2003
Fabric or leather upholstery, maple or
beech frame.
H 32¼", W 22", D 22½" (82 x 56 x 57 cm)
Producer: Getama (Photo: Erik Brahl)

2-151

2-152

2-151
W Chair
Design: Pentti Hakala, 1988
Lacquered birch backrest, steel tubing
frame, leather seat.
H 31¼", W 16¼", D 19¼" (79 x 41 x 49 cm)
Producer: HKT Korhonen

2-152
Dale
Design: Antti Kotilainen, 2002
High curving back of molded plywood in
several finishes, concealed frame, elliptical
steel tubing legs, powder-coated chrome
or matte chrome finish. Optional seat pad.
H 33½", W 21", D 20¾" (85 x 53.5 x 53 cm)
Producer: Piiroinen

2-153
Una
Design: Timo Saarnio, 2004
One-piece form-pressed birch or beech
veneer, lacquered, stained, or waxed;
available with upholstered seat pad, metal
armrests.
H 32", W 23", D 21" (81 x 58 x 53 cm)
Producer: Martela

2-153

2-154

2-154
Rodrigo
Design: Mårten Claesson, 2003
Natural birch, birch/walnut, walnut, or
lacquered shell; tubular metal base.
H 31½", W 18¾", D 20¼" (80 x 48 x 52 cm)
Producer: Swedese

2-155
#8002 Series Chair
Design: Rud Thygesen & Johnny Sørensen,
1978
Laminated beech, made without screws or
dowels; linoleum, laminate, wood slat or
upholstered seat; available in three back
heights and several variations or backless;
matching stools, tables, and children's versions also available.
Seat: H 17¼ or 16¼", Diam 16"
(41 or 44 cm)
Producer: Magnus Olesen

2-155b

2-155a

2-156

2-157

2-158

2-156
Sola
Design: Teemu Järvi, 2005
Form-pressed plywood seat and back, natural or
stained birch, oak or ash, or upholstered, chrome-plated or powder-
coated tubular steel frame.
H 30½", W 19½", D 20½" (77 x 49.5 x 52 cm)
Producer: HKT Korhonen

2-157
#4575 Bird Armchair
Design: Ralf Lindberg.
Laminated beech, birch, or oak veneer seat,
natural or stained, tubular steel frame.
H 31½", W 22¾", D 19¾" (80 x 58 x 50 cm)
Producer: Gärsnäs

2-158
#S-020 Torro
Design: Jonas Lindvall, 2004
Birch or oak, natural or stained finish, tubular steel frame.
H 30", W 18½", D 19¾" (76 x 47 x 50 cm)
Producer: Skandiform

2-159b

2-159a

2-159
Qvintus
Design: Johannes Foersom and Peter Hiort-Lorenzen, 1995
Form-pressed back, natural birch or beech or stain finish,
powder-coated or chrome-plated steel frame.
H 30¼", W 23¼", D 20¾" (77 x 59 x 53 cm)
Producer: Lammhults

2-160
Puma
Design: Komplot Design, 1996
Natural or stained birch, fabric, or leather seat, tubular steel
frame.
H 32¼", W 17¾", D 20½" (82 x 45 x 52 cm)
Producer: Källemo

2-160

2-161
Kiss
Design: Sari Anttonen, 1998
Injection-molded polyurethane, tubular
steel legs.
H 32¾", W 18", D 21¾" (83 x 46 x 55 cm)
Producer: Piiroinen

2-162
Cornflake
Design: Claesson Koivisto Rune, 2001
Natural, stained, or lacquer finish
laminated plywood or upholstered seat,
chrome-plated or silver-lacquered tubular
metal legs.
H 32", W 20", D 19¾" (81 x 51 x 50 cm)
Producer: Offecct (Photo: Peter Fotograf)

2-163
Fold
Design: Märten Claesson, 2005
Laminated birch veneer, chrome-plated
or silver-lacquered steel legs; companion
upholstered sectional chair, stool, linking
tables.
H 30", W 21", D 21¼" (76 x 53 x 54 cm)
Producer: Swedese

2-161

2-162

2-163

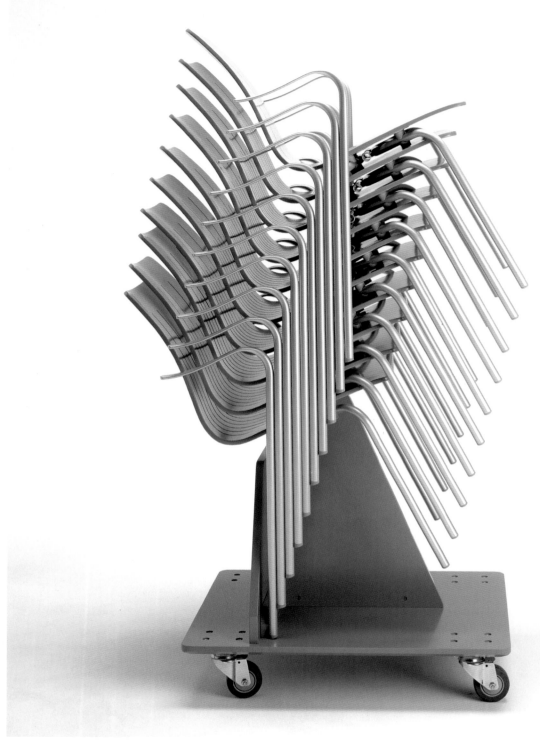

2-164

2-164
#9871 Armchair
Design: Bernt, 1998
Beech, maple, or ash, chrome-plated or
powder-lacquered steel frame.
H 33", W 20¾", D 21½" (84 x 53 x 54 cm)
Producer: Getama (Photo: Erik Brahl)

2-165
Siro
Design: Juoko Järvisalo, 2001
Molded birch plywood shell, natural,
stained, or upholstered in fabric or leather,
square tubular steel legs.
H 32¼", W 20", D 21¼" (82 x 51 x 54 cm)
Producer: Mobel (Photo: Jussi Tiainen)

2-166
Gubi Chair
Design: Komplot Design, 2003
Seat and back formed with 3-D veneer
molding technique, beech, maple, oak, or
walnut veneer, polished or matte chrome-
plated base; available as lounge chair
with wood legs and upholstered seat, or
barstool.
H 32¾", W 19¾", D 21¾" (83 x 50 x 55 cm)
Producer: Gubi

2-165

2-166a

2-166b

2-167a

2-167b

2-168

2-167
Pilo Maximal (left), Pilo Oval (right)
Design: Komplot Design, 1996
Solid wood frame, laminated with birch or
beech veneer.
H 30¼", W 19¾", D 19" (77 x 50 x 48 cm)
Producer: Swedese

2-168
Citra
Design: Tord Björkland, 2005
Laminated beech, birch, or black-stained
beech veneer, black or light gray tubular
metal frame; optional back opening; avail-
able with upholstered seat.
H 34¼", W 17¼", D 20½" (87 x 44 x 52 cm)
Producer: Kinnarps

2-169

2-169
Parts of a Rainbow
Design: Christian Flindt, 2005
Set of ten varicolored chairs, Repsol glass,designed to use individually, stack sideways as a bench, or stack as a wall.
Producer: Flindt Design (Photo: Magnus Klitten)

DESK CHAIRS

2-171

Previous page
2-170
#3117, #3217, #3137
Design: Arne Jacobsen, 1955
Fabric over veneered shell; with or without arms, steel swivel base, optional casters.
H 30", W 19¾" (with arms 23½"), D 20½"
(76 x 50 or 60 x 52 cm)
Producer: Fritz Hansen

This page
2-171
Cobra
Design: Mattias Ljunggren, 2003
Leather over cold-foam seat and back, molded aluminum base, wood armrests; available with fabric upholstery.
H 35–39¾", W 23½", D 23½"
(89–101 x 60 x 60 cm)
Producer: Källemo

2-172
EJ 205 Flamingo
Design: Johannes Foersom and Peter
Hiort-Lorenzen, 2003
Leather or fabric fixed covers over
molded polyurethane foam, chrome-
plated stainless steel pedestal base;
available with four legs and casters.
H 25½", W 25½", D 23½"
(65 x 65 x 60 cm)
Producer: Erik Jørgensen

2-173
#2003 Kevi
Design: Jørgen Rasmussen, 1973
Molded veneer seat and back, natural
beech or colored lacquer, polished
aluminum glide or cater base; available
with arms or backless, in three heights.
H 19¾, 23½, or 27½", W 18½", D 13¾"
(50, 60, 70 x 47 x 35 cm)
Producer: Fritz Hansen

2-172

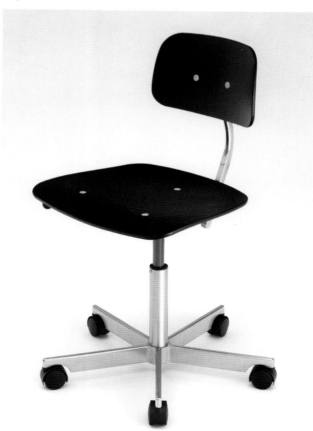

2-173

2-174

2-174
PP 502
Design: Hans J. Wegner, 1955
Oak, ash, mahogany, or cherry with leather, steel swivel base, casters.
H 28¾", W 29¼", D 21¾" (73 x 74 x 55 cm)
Producer: PP Møbler

2-175

2-176

2-175
#8106 Capisco
Design: Peter Opsvik, 1984
Upholstery over foam, adjustable
metal swivel base on casters.
H 17¼", D 14½–18" (44 x 37–46 cm)
Producer: Håg

2-176
03 Sirkus
Design: Yrjö Kukkapuro, 1983
Seat shell of formed birch plywood faced
in melamine laminate or upholstered.
H 30–36½", W 17", D 20" (76–92.5 x 43 x 51 cm)
Producer: Avarte

2-177
#455 Fysio
Design: Yrjö Kukkapuro, 1978
Formed birch plywood shell and armrests,
adjustable chrome-plated steel swivel base;
available as conference, desk, or lounge chair
with headrest.
H 43¾", W 23¾", D 23¼" (111 x 60 x 59 cm)
Producer: Avarte

2-177

2-178

2-178
Jobb-2
Design: Yrjö Wiherheimo and
Pekka Kojo, 2000
Ergonomic chair, leather upholstery,
steel frame; available in three back
heights, fully adjustable, with movable
armrests, varying lumbar and shoulder
support as user changes position. Also
available with rigid frame.
H 17¾–22½", W 23½", D 23½"
(45–57 x 60 x 60 cm)
Producer: Vivero

2-179

2-179
U-turn
Design: Lotte Olesen & Peter Kristiansen,
2003
Laminated wood frame, chrome auto-
return swivel base, leather or fabric uphol-
stery. Matching table available.
H 26", W 22" D 18" (66 x 56 x 46 cm)
Producer: Magnus Olesen

2-180
#3271 Oxford
Design: Arne Jacobsen, 1965
Leather or fabric upholstery over polyurethane foam on molded wood shell,
satin-polished aluminum frame; also available without arms, with high back, with
swivel-tilt mechanism, or as desk chair on
casters.
H 35¾", W 19¾", D 26" (91 x 50 x 66 cm)
Producer: Fritz Hansen

2-180

SOFAS, LOVE SEATS, CHAISES, & SECTIONALS

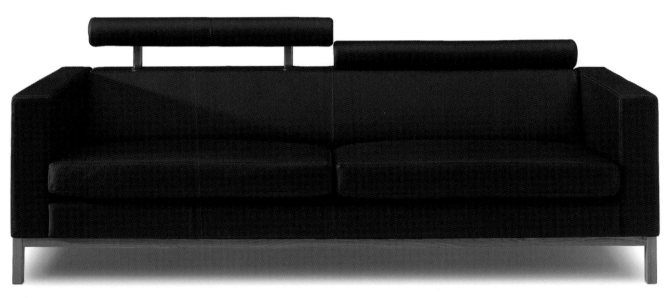

2-181

2-182
Man
Design: Norway Says, 2005
Fabric over polyurethane foam and fiber,
wood frame, satin or polished-chrome
finish steel base. Available with chaise
section.
Dimensions: H 24", W 98", D 38¾"
(61 x 250 x 98 cm)
Producer L. K. Hjelle

2-182a

2-182b

Previous page
2-181
Tube
Design: C. H. Spak, 2004
Upholstery over foam, wood frame and legs, pull-up
tubular neckrest.
H 31½", W 88 ½", D 31¾" (80 x 224 x 81 cm)
Producer: Swedese

2-183
6203 Neptunus
Design: Åke Axelsson
Fabric upholstery,
natural birch or oak frame.
L 63" or 74¾" (160 or 190 cm)
Producer: Gärsnäs

2-183

2-184

2-184
Radius
Design: Philip Bro Ludvigsen, 2004
Upholstered modular units for curved,
circular, or serpentine seating arrange-
ments, chrome pedestals; wedge or half-
round sections, optional armrests,
recliners, and side tables.
Producer: Eilersen

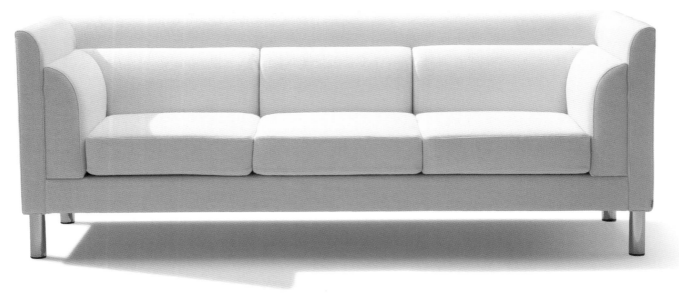

2-185

2-186

2-187a

Opposite
2-185
Liva
Design: Pelikan Design, 1996
Fabric or leather upholstery, solid natural-
finish beech or chrome legs; available as
two or three-seat sofa, with modules to
form corner units.
Producer: Fora Form

2-186
PK-31/3
Design: Poul Kjærholm, 1958
Leather upholstery, steel frame; also avail-
able as two-seat sofa or armchair.
H 30", L 78", D 30" (76 x 198 x 76 cm)
Producer: Fritz Hansen

This page
2-187
EJ 20
Design: Jørgen Gammelgaard, 1985
Rigid shell, soft removable cushions,
beech, beech/mahogany, or chrome-plated
steel legs; available as two- or three-seat
sofa or armchair.
H 29½", L 56 or 79½", D 31"
(75 x 142 or 202 x 79 cm)
Producer: Erik Jørgensen

2-187b

2-188

2-188
EJ 800 Rotor
Design: Johannes Foersom and Peter Hiort-Lorenzen, 1983
Fabric or leather over molded polyurethane foam, chrome-plated steel frame, pivoting back; available as chaise or two-seat sofa .
H 32¼", L 59", D 30" (82 x 150 x 77 cm)
Producer: Erik Jørgensen

2-189
EJ 900 Pipeline
Design: Johannes Foersom and Peter Hiort-Lorenzen, 1987
Molded polyurethane foam, black lacquered frame, polished or matte chrome-plated metal legs; available in various sizes and configurations.
Producer: Erik Jørgensen

2-189

2-190

2-191

2-190
Yesbox
Design: Yrjö Wiherheimo, 2006
Seating system. Fabric over foam, tubular
steel base and legs.
Individual modular units, with or without
arms, with individual bases or multi-unit
integrated tubular base.
Producer: Vivero

2-191
EJ 2800
Seesaw
Design: Louise Campbell, 2003
Wool upholstery over cold-cured
polyurethane foam, wood frame.
H 26¾", L 95¾" (68 x 243 cm)
Producer: Erik Jørgensen

2-192a

2-192b

2-192
EJ 600
Design: Erik Jørgensen, 1984
Fixed covers over cold-cured polyurethane foam; lacquered aluminum or beech legs. Matching ottoman.
H 28½", L 74¾ or 92½", D 34¾"
(72 x 190 or 235 x 88 cm)
Producer: Erik Jørgensen

Opposite
2-193
EJ 2100 Meadow
Design: Johannes Foersom and Peter Hiort-Lorenzen, 2001
Removable covers over molded polyurethane foam, no-sag springs and pocket springs; matte chrome-plated steel legs.
H 30¼", L 64 or 93", D 34"
(77 x 162.5 or 236 x 86.5 cm)
Producer: Erik Jørgensen

2-194
Butterfly
Design: Alice Kunftova, 1992
Fabric over bentwood, metal seat frame with Pullmaflex, foam, and Hollofill; cast aluminum legs; available as chaise. Coordinating chairs also available.
H 31", L 68", D 29" (79 x 173 x 74 cm)
Producer: Källemo

2-193

2-194

2-195

2-195
Cyklop
Design: Dan Ihreborn, 1996
Down and polyurethane upholstery,
curved back and seat, chrome-plated
steel legs.
L 86" (220 cm)
Producer: Kallin & Franzén
(Move-range)

2-196
EJ 60
Design: Johannes Foersom and
Peter Hiort-Lorenzen, 1998
Fabric over molded polyurethane foam,
foam cushions, matte chrome-plated
steel legs.
H 29½", L 33, 60¼, or 86¼", D 32¼"
(75 x 84, 153, or 219 x 82 cm)
Producer: Erik Jørgensen

2-196

2-197
E-seat
Design: Thomas Eriksson, 2002
Fabric over cold-foam fill, wood frame
with Nozag spring system,
chrome-plated steel runners.
H 28¾", L 66", D 26"
(73 x 168 x 66 cm)
Producer: Offecct
(Photo: Peter Fotograf)

2-198
Wing
Design: Dan Ihreborn, 2002
Fabric over foam and down,
chrome-plated steel legs.
H 30¾", L 95", D 30¾"
(78 x 240 x 78 cm)
Producer: Kallin and Franzén
(Move-range)

2-199
Float
Design: Eero Koivisto, 2005
Fabric or leather over cold-foam fill, wood
frame with Nozag spring system, mirror
laminate on base.
H 28¾", L 66" D 26" (73 x 168 x 66 cm)
Producer: Offecct

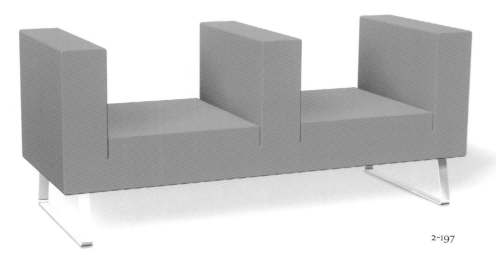

2-197

2-198

2-199

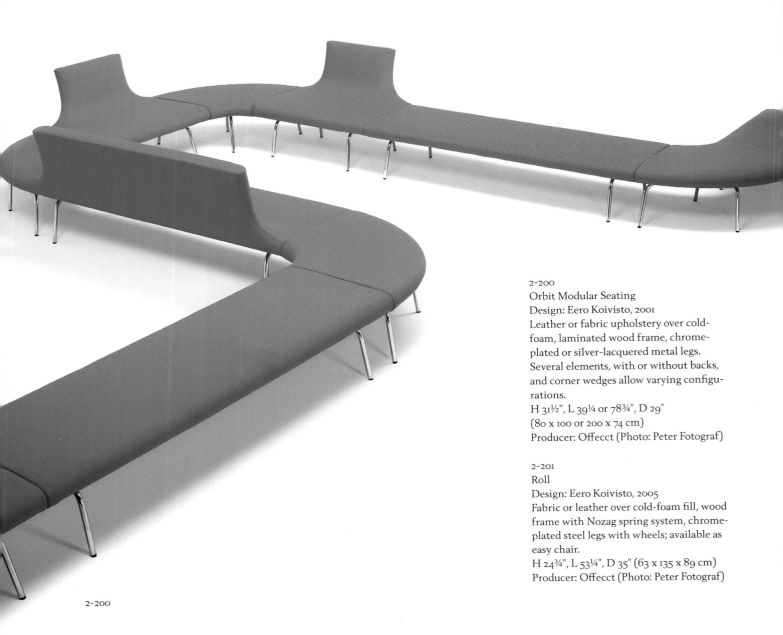

2-200

2-200
Orbit Modular Seating
Design: Eero Koivisto, 2001
Leather or fabric upholstery over cold-foam, laminated wood frame, chrome-plated or silver-lacquered metal legs. Several elements, with or without backs, and corner wedges allow varying configurations.
H 31½", L 39¼ or 78¾", D 29"
(80 x 100 or 200 x 74 cm)
Producer: Offecct (Photo: Peter Fotograf)

2-201
Roll
Design: Eero Koivisto, 2005
Fabric or leather over cold-foam fill, wood frame with Nozag spring system, chrome-plated steel legs with wheels; available as easy chair.
H 24¾", L 53¼", D 35" (63 x 135 x 89 cm)
Producer: Offecct (Photo: Peter Fotograf)

2-201

2-202

2-203

2-202
Backslash
Design: Jens Juul Eilersen, 2005
Fabric or leather upholstery, with or without cushions, polished steel or wood legs; available as one-piece sofa or sectional elements in several sizes, and corner chaise.
Each section: H 25", L 51–74¾", D 41¾ or 47½" (64 x 130–190 x 106 or 121 cm)
Producer: Eilersen

2-203
Slide
Design: Eero Koivisto, 2005
Fabric or leather over cold-foam, wood frame with Nozag spring system, steel legs; available as lounge chair.
H 25½", L 58", D 35" (65 x 147 x 89 cm)
Producer: Offecct (Photo: Peter Fotograf)

2-204a

2-204b

2-204
Domino
Design: Jens Juul Eilersen, 2001
Fabric or leather over foam and fiberfill, steel base; modular system, available in twenty-five elements of different depths and widths, with or without arms, with matching ottomans, extra back and neck pillows, removable covers. Tables also available.
H 25", L 71, 82½, or 94½", D 43"
(64 x 180, 210, or 240 x 110 cm)
Producer: Eilersen

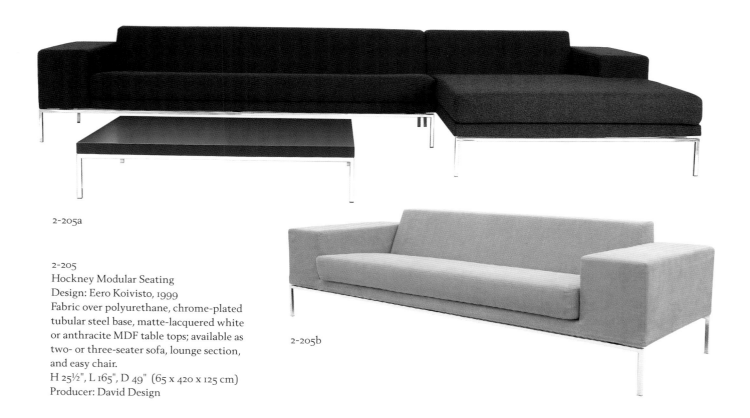

2-205a

2-205
Hockney Modular Seating
Design: Eero Koivisto, 1999
Fabric over polyurethane, chrome-plated
tubular steel base, matte-lacquered white
or anthracite MDF table tops; available as
two- or three-seater sofa, lounge section,
and easy chair.
H 25½", L 165", D 49" (65 x 420 x 125 cm)
Producer: David Design

2-205b

2-206
Loveseat Lounge
Design: Riikka Paasonen & Petra Majantie,
2000
Nylon upholstery, aluminum frame.
H 13¾", L 94½", D 47¼" (35 x 240 x 120 cm)
Producer: Formverk

2-206

2-207a

2-207b

2-207
#302½ (Sofa); 303 (Loveseat)
Design: Andreas Hansen, 1998
Fabric upholstery over foam, ash, oak, or
American cherry frame.
H 34", L 84¾ or 72", D 27"
(87 x 215 or 183 x 70 cm)
Producer: Brdr-Andersen

2-208
Zigzag
Design: Andreas Hansen, 2004
Fabric or leather upholstery, polished or matte
chrome-plated metal legs; modular based on
hexagonal forms using five basic elements,
including sofa and chair sections.
Sofa: H 26", L 78¾", D 28" (66 x 200 x 72 cm)
Producer: Eilersen

2-208

2-209
Ateljee
Design: Yrjö Kukkapuro, 1964
Birch veneer or black-stained plywood
seat and back, detachable upholstery and
cushions, tubular steel legs; available as
two- or three-seat sofa or chair, optional
neck support.
H 28½", L 32¾, 37¾, or 63¼", D 32¾"
(72 x 83, 96, 161, or 226 x 83.5 cm)
Producer: Avarte

2-210
Century 2000
Design: Hans J. Wegner, 2000
Fabric or leather upholstery on wood
frame, metal legs.
H 28¾", L 61, 74¾, or 86½", D 32"
(73 x 155, 190, or 220 x 81 cm)
Producer: Getama (Photo: Erik Brahl)

2-209a

2-209b

2-210

2-211

2-212

Opposite

2-211
280 Modular
Design: Hans J. Wegner, 1980
Fabric or leather upholstery, beech or oak frame and legs.
H 30¾", L 24¾ or 30" (each unit), D 30"
(78 x 63 or 76 x 76)
Producer: Getama (Photo: Erik Brahl)

2-212
285
Design: Hans J. Wegner, 1985
Fabric or leather upholstery,
beech or oak frame and legs.
H 29¼", L 50½ or 72¾", D 28"
(74 x 128 or 185 x 71 cm)
Producer: Getama (Photo: Erik Brahl)

This page

2-213
Break
Design: Norway Says, 2004
Leather upholstery over polyurethane foam,
plywood frame, satin or high-polish chrome-steel base.
H 28¾", L 72¾", D 30" (73 x 76 x 185 cm)
Producer: LK Hjelle

2-214
Quadratus
Design: Åke Axelsson, 2005
Fabric upholstery over birch and stainless steel frame; modular units
combine into square and rectangular configurations.
Each unit: H 31", L 23½", D 23½"
(79 x 60 x 60 cm)
Producer: Gärsnäs

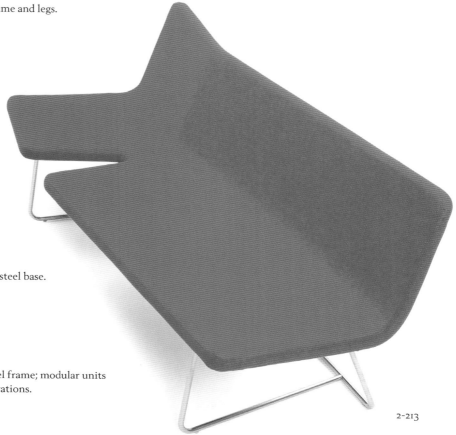

2-213

2-214

2-215

2-216

This page
2-215
Hal
Design: Norway Says, 2003
Upholstery over polyurethane foam, wood frame,
satin-finish or polished chrome-plated steel base.
H 31½", L 39¼, 78¾, or 90½", D 31½"
(80 x 100, 200 or 230 x 80 cm)
Producer: LK Hjelle

2-216
Ugo
Design: Norway Says, 2003
Wood frame, polyurethane foam,
satin-finish or polished chrome-plated steel base.
H 27¼", L 89½", D 32¼" (69 x 227 x 82 cm)
Producer: LK Hjelle

Opposite
2-217
Kennedy
Design: Anki Gneib, 2003
Fabric upholstery over cold-foam seat and back,
wood frame with Nozag spring system, solid oak legs.
H 26¾", L 95", D 35½" (73 x 241 x 90 cm)
Producer: Offecct (Photo: Peter Fotograf)

2-218
PP 932-3
Design: Soren Ulrik Petersen, 2002
Fabric upholstery over foam, wood frame detailing and base; available in several sizes, with various leg treatments and wood trims.
H 25", L 62", D 33+6" (frame) (63.5 x 157 x 84+15 cm)
Producer: PP Møbler

2-217

2-218

2-219

2-220

2-219
Tops
Design: Jens Juul Eilersen, 2002
Fabric or leather upholstery, reversible seat cushions, polished
chrome-plated legs; removable frame cover available.
H 32", L 78¾ or 98", D 98¼" (81 x 200 or 250 cm)
Producer: Eilersen

2-220
EJ 600-Landscape Modular Sofa
Design: Erik Jørgensen, 1996
Fixed fabric cushions over cold-cured polyurethane foam, lacquered
aluminum or beech legs; available with or without arms, to arrange
in various configurations.
Basic unit: H 28½", L 74¾ or 92½", D 34¾" (72 x 90 or 235 x 88 cm)
Producer: Erik Jørgensen

2-221
Cut Modular Seating
Design: Tom Stepp
Leather or fabric upholstery over cut-
foam, movable loose cushions, wood frame
with black-tipped, chrome-plated metal
legs. Corner units, right and left modules,
chair, and ottoman; components joined by
locking system.
Basic unit: H 31½", L 38¼ or 47¼", D 30¾"
(80 x 97 or 120 x 78 cm)
Producer: Fredericia

2-222
PK-80
Design: Poul Kjærholm, 1958
Leather seat and back, steel frame.
H 11¾", L 75", W 31½" (30 x 190 x 80 cm)
Producer: Fritz Hansen

2-223
Ziggi
Design: Flemming Busk
Daybed, channeled upholstery over foam,
stainless steel legs, oak, maple, or walnut.
tray table.
H 14", L 79", D 31" (36 x 200 x 80 cm)
Producer: Globe

2-221

2-222

2-223

2-224

2-225

2-224
Spoke-back Sofa
Design: Børge Mogensen, 1945
Fabric cushion, beech, oak, sycamore, or walnut frame, drop-down sides
and leather straps.
H 34", L 63–75", D 28¾" (86 x 160–190 x 73 cm)
Producer: Fredericia

2-225
Low-cut
Design: Anne Louise Due de Foenn
Fabric or leather upholstery over foam, stainless steel, available in two-
or three-seat versions.
H 28¼", L 108¼", D 39¼" (72 x 275 x 100 cm)
Producer: Globe

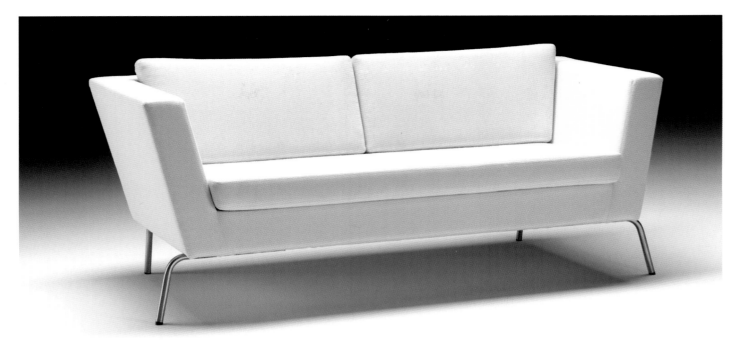

2-226

2-226
#9209 Wide
Design: Tom Stepp, 2003
Fabric or microfiber upholstery over foam,
brushed stainless steel frame.
H 34¼", L 69 or 78¾", D 19¾"
(87 x 175 or 200 x 50 cm)
Producer: Stouby

2-227
#9830 Jass
Design: Tom Stepp, 2005
Fabric or leather upholstery, brushed
aluminum frame; available as chair with
swivel base.
H 32¾", L 57¾", D 36" (83 x 147 x 93 cm)
Producer: Stouby

2-227

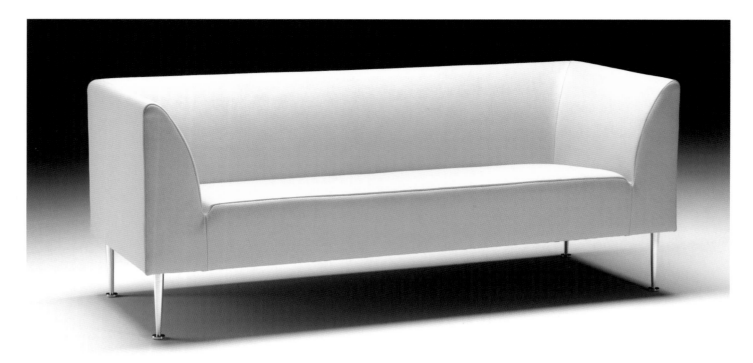

2-228

2-229

2-230

2-231

Opposite
2-228
#9812 Cubo
Design: Hans Thyge Raunkjaer, 1999
Leather, fabric or microfiber upholstery over cold-foam and pocket springs, wood frame, aluminum, beech or cherry legs; available as two- or three-seat sofa, arm chair, or footstool.
H 29½", L 55½ or 71¼", D 27" (75 x 141 or 181 x 69 cm)
Producer: Stouby

2-229
#9822 Time Out
Design: Tom Stepp, 2001
Fabric or microfiber upholstery over cold-foam and pocket springs, wood frame, chrome legs; available as two- or three-seat sofa, chair, or footstool. Adjustable seats with optional electric controls.
H 31½", L 78¾ or 90½", D 41¼" (80 x 200 or 230 x 105 cm)
Producer: Stouby

This page
2-230
#9823 Mojo
Design: Hans Thyge Raunkjaer, 2002
Microfiber upholstery over cold-foam and pocket springs, with soft or firm back cushions, wood frame, brushed aluminum legs; available in straight or corner sections.
H 31½", L 88", D 37" (80 x 224 x 95 cm)
Producer: Stouby

2-231
Lotus
Design: Flemming Busk + Stephan B. Hertzog
Upholstered shell, stainless metal frame; matching chair, swivel chair, table.
H 29½", L 76½", D 25½" (75 x 195 x 65 cm)
Producer: Globe

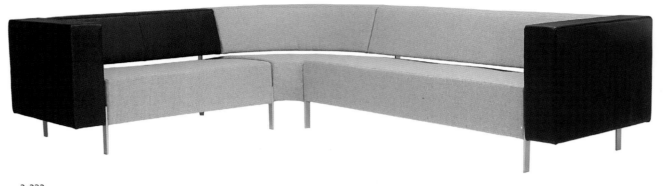

2-232

2-233

2-232
Pio
Design: Dan Ihreborn, 2003
Modular seating units with slit back, to arrange freestanding or
against a wall; fabric upholstery over soft foam, polished grey metal
framework; available as two or three-seat sofa or chair, also with
curved sections.
H 28", L 29½"–80" (six sizes), D 34½" (73 x 75–204 x 88 cm)
Producer: Kinnarps

2-233
Trix
Design: Dan Ihreborn, 1996
Modular seating units in curved configurations. Fabric upholstery
over foam black or light gray tubular metal frame. Coordinated
chair.
H 30¼", D 37½" (77 x 95 cm)
Producer: Kinnarps

2-234
#3321 Swan Sofa
Design: Arne Jacobsen, 1958
Natural leather on molded polystyrene,
cast aluminum base.
H 31", L 56¾", D 29 ¼" (79 x 144 x 74 cm)
Producer: Fritz Hansen

2-235
Avec
Design: Birgitta Lööf
Fabric upholstery over polyester filling, blockboard
structure, fold-down sides, tubular steel legs.
H 33", L 80", D 27¾" (84 x 203 x 70 cm)
Producer: Klaessons

2-234

2-235

2-236

2-237

2-236
250 Eshu
Design: Roger Sveian, 2002
Fabric upholstery over foam, tubular metal frame.
H 30", L 98½, 86½, or 51¼", D 35½" (76 x 250, 220 or 130 x 90 cm)
Producer: Mokasser (formerly Leads)

2-237
#FJ 4100 Poet
Design: Finn Juhl, 1941
Handsewn fabric upholstery, legs available in various woods.
H 34¼", L 53½", D 31½" (87 x 136 x 80 cm)
Producer: Hansen & Sorensen

2-238

2-238
Apollo
Design: Martin Haksteen, 1997
Fabric upholstery over foam, wood frame
and legs.
H 34¾", L 78¾ or 86½"
(88, 200, or 220 x 91 cm)
Producer: LK Hjelle

2-239

2-239
Kavaljier
Design: Karl-Erik Ekselius, 1997
Fabric upholstery over foam; flexible modular system available as
two- or three-seat straight sofa or as 45- and 90-degree-angle wedges
for various curved configurations.
Producer: EFG

2-240
Kamon
Design: Moni Beuchel, 2006
Fabric or leather upholstery, oak frame.
Matching bench available.
H 29", W 51", D 26" (75 x 130 x 66 cm)
Producer: Karl Andersson

2-241
#9603 Don Don
Design: Tom Stepp, 1998
Leather, fabric, or microfiber upholstery
over cold foam and pocket springs, wood
frame, stained beech or aluminum legs
and front wheels. Matching chair available.
Dimensions: H 32¼", W 86¼", D 36¾"
(82 x 219 x 93 cm)
Producer: Stouby

2-242
Playback
Design: Eero Koivisto, 2003
Flexible seating system with curved sec-
tions, wood frame, fabric upholstery over
foam and no-sag springs, multi-cushion
back, chrome-plated steel legs.
Producer: Offecct

2-240

2-241

2-242

2-243

2-243
Planet Sofa
Design: Sven Ivar Dysthe, 1965
Stretch fabric upholstery, wood frame.
Companion to classic chair.
Producer: Fora Form

2-244a

2-244
Cloud
Design: Marten Claesson, 2003
Fabric upholstery over high-resilience foam
on Pullmaflex, solid wood frame, chrome-
finish or lacquered silver gray steel legs.
Matching chair.
Sofa: H 31½", L 112½ or 45¾", D 36½"
(80 x 286 or 116 x 93 cm)
Producer: Swedese

2-245
Decision
Design: Pelikan Design, 1986
Modular seating system in several shapes to
assemble in straight, curved, or angular con-
figurations; coordinating tables and wedge
cushions.
Producer: Fritz Hansen

2-244b

2-245

2-246

2-246
Tamariu
Design: Harri Korhonen, 1999
Fixed or loose fabric upholstery over
feather and Superlon, steel springs, wood
frame and legs.
H 30", L 34¾, 57½, or 80¼", D 37½" (76 x
88, 146, or 204 x 95 cm)
Producer: Inno

2-247
Fridhem
Design: Kristian Eriksson, 1999
Fabric upholstery, wood frame; also avail-
able as armchair.
H 35½", L 69 or 76¾", D 35½"
(90 x 175 or 195 x 90 cm)
Producer: G.A.D.

2-247

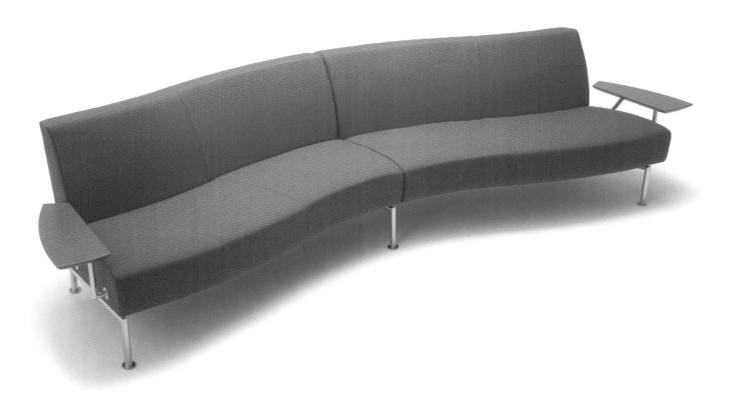

2-248

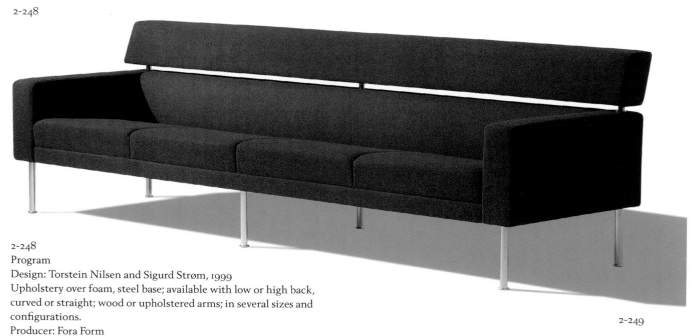

2-248
Program
Design: Torstein Nilsen and Sigurd Strøm, 1999
Upholstery over foam, steel base; available with low or high back,
curved or straight; wood or upholstered arms; in several sizes and
configurations.
Producer: Fora Form

2-249

2-249
Distance
Design: Niels Jørgen Haugesen, 2004
Fabric upholstery over hardwood frame; steel legs; available in two-,
three-, and four-seat versions; also as corner unit, armchair, and
stool.
H 30", L 90", D 31" (76 x 229 x 79 cm)
Producer: Fredericia

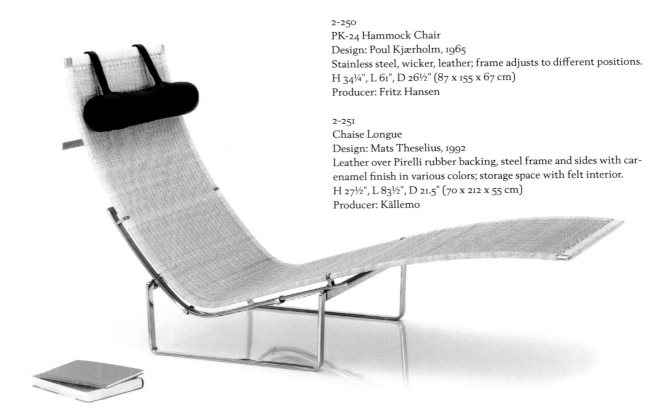

2-250
PK-24 Hammock Chair
Design: Poul Kjærholm, 1965
Stainless steel, wicker, leather; frame adjusts to different positions.
H 34¼", L 61", D 26½" (87 x 155 x 67 cm)
Producer: Fritz Hansen

2-251
Chaise Longue
Design: Mats Theselius, 1992
Leather over Pirelli rubber backing, steel frame and sides with car-enamel finish in various colors; storage space with felt interior.
H 27½", L 83½", D 21.5" (70 x 212 x 55 cm)
Producer: Källemo

2-250

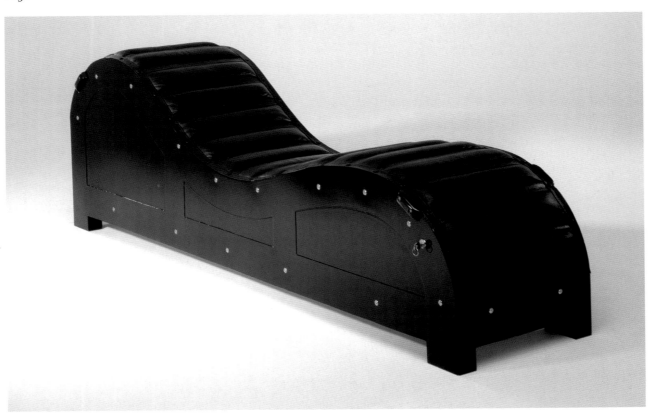

2-251

2-252

2-252
Concave
Design: Jonas Bohlin, 1983
Upholstery over foam seat and pillow, bentwood frame, foam seat
and pillow, black steel base.
H 17¾", L 86.5", D 19¾" (45 x 220 x 50 cm)
Producer: Källemo

2-253
PP 524 Deck Chair
Design: Hans J. Wegner, 1958
Ash or oak, string back and seat, neck cushion, sheepskin (not
shown); adjustable back.
H 35", L 62–67", W 25" (89 x 157–170 x 63.5 cm)
Producer: PP Møbler

2-253

2-254

2-254
Control Adjustable Recliner
Design: Jens Juul Eilersen, 1985
Leather or fabric upholstery over foam
and fiberfill, chrome-plated steel base,
optional neck pillow and wheels; neck,
back and foot sections individually adjustable.
W 33½" x L 72¾" or W 27½" x L 71¾" [ck]
(85 x 85 or 70 x 182 cm)
Producer: Eilersen

2-255
Deck Chair
Design: Bernt, 1960
Natural-tone cotton channel-stitched
cushions, ash and mahogany frame, adjust-
able backrest.
Producer: C. N. Jørgensens

2-255

2-256
#2240 Sun Lounger
Design: Arne Vodder, 2001
Wood on sand-blasted stainless steel frame
with wheels.
H 12½", L 71", D 23½" (32 x 180 x 60 cm)
Producer: Kircodan

2-257
Lounge
Design: Bernt
Ash frame, natural-tone cotton fabric
cushions.
Producer: C. N. Jørgensens

2-256

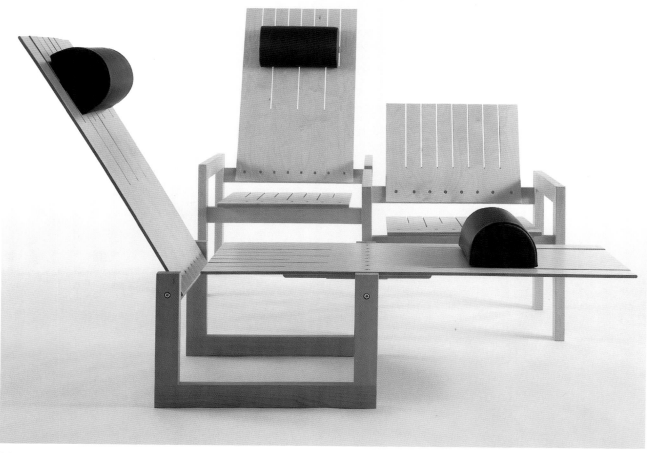

2-257

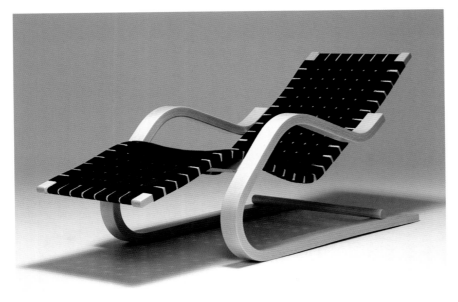

2-258

2-258
#43 Lounge Chair
Design: Alvar Aalto, 1936-37
Natural lacquered birch frame, woven seat
of linen webbing or black leather belting.
H 41", L 64½", D 33¼" (104 x 164 x 85 cm)
Producer: Artek

2-259
#7513 Lounge
Design: Rud Thygesen & Johnny Sørensen,
1984
Laminated beech, cherry, oak, mahogany,
sycamore or walnut, with leather and fab-
ric upholstery.
H 30" x L 62¼" x D 21½" (76 x 158 x 55 cm)
Producer: Fredericia

2-260
Woob
Design: Eero Koivisto, 2005
Fabric upholstery over cold-foam, lami-
nated wood frame with chrome-plated
steel support.
H 31½", L 66½", D 31½" (90 x 160 x 80 cm)
Producer: Offecct

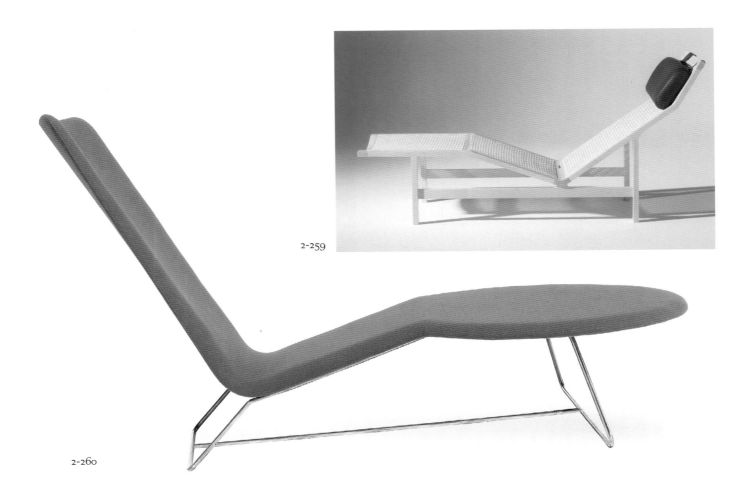

2-259

2-260

2-261
Newport
Design: Johannes Foersom and Peter Hiort-
Lorenzen, 1988
Fabric upholstery over foam, steel frame and
legs; optional armrests or attached steel mini-
tables.
H 33½ or 45¼"; L 64¾ or 92";
D 31½, 35½, or 40"
(85 or 115 x 156, 162 or 234 x 80, 90 or 100 cm)
Producer: Lammhults

2-262
Milo
Design: Jouko Järvisalo, 2003
Fabric or leather over foam, wood and steel
frame, solid wood and plywood seat and back,
chrome, black, or gray steel or white alumi-
num legs; available in two- or three-seat or
single chair versions, with or without arms.
Matching bench.
H 27½", L 31¼, 60, or 82", D 29"
(70 x 79.5, 152.5, or 209 x 74.5 cm)
Producer: Mobel

2-261

2-262

BENCHES & STOOLS

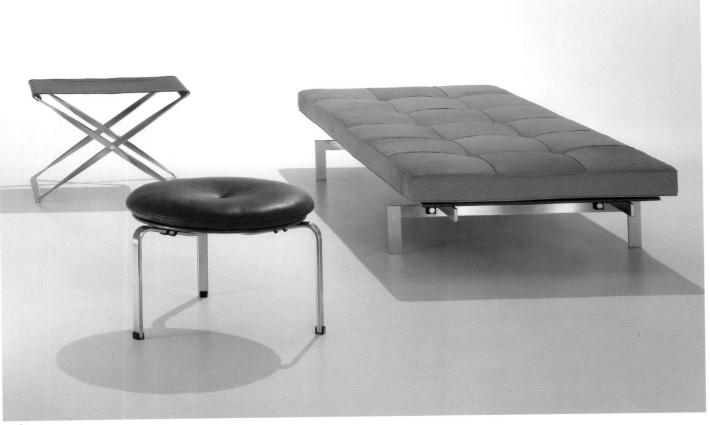

2-264

2-264
PK-91, PK-80, PK-33
Design: Poul Kjærholm, 1958
Folding stool, long bench, and two-legged round stool,
leather on stainless steel frames.
Folding stool: H 14½", W 23½", D 17¾" (37 x 60 x 45 cm)
Long bench: H 11¾", W 75", D 31½" (30 x 190 x 80 cm)
Round stool: H 13½", Diam. 20¾" (34, 53 cm)
Producer: Fritz Hansen

Previous page
2-263
X-base Stool
Design: Preben Fabricius and Jørgen Kastholm,
1965
Leather, stainless steel.
Producer: Bo-Ex

2-265

2-265
CH 54
Design: Hans J. Wegner, 1966
Beech or oak frame with leather or fabric
upholstery.
H 17¼", W 19¾", D 15¾" (44 x 50 x 40 cm)
Producer: Carl Hansen
(Photo: Søren Larson)

2-266

2-266
Anna Stool
Design: Anna Kraitz, 2001
Molded leather on chrome-plated steel.
Producer: Källemo

2-267

2-268

2-267
Bill, Bull, and Bob
Design: Team Johanson
Multipurpose cube-, drum-, or prism-shaped ottomans with fabric or leather upholstery over rigid frame.
All H 17 ½" (44 cm)
Producer: Johanson Design

2-268
Boy
Design: Norway Says, 2005
Fabric upholstery over foam, wood frame.
H 19", W 19", D 16½" (48 x 48 x 42 cm)
Producer: LK Hjelle

2-269

2-269
Flower Stools
Design: Eero Koivisto, 2004
Red, orange, white, or black cold-foam
with polyurethane surface.
H 17¼", Diam. 21¼" (44, 54 cm)
Producer: Offecct (Photo: Peter Fotograf)

2-270

2-271

2-270
Tale Stool
Design: Ilmari Tapiovaara, 1953
Plywood veneer seat birch (various finishes), teak, walnut, or oak;
birch (various finishes) or oak base; stackable.
H 15¾", W 26½" (40 x 67 cm)
Producer: Aero

2-271
Voxia Collection-VUW
Design: Peter Karpf, 2001
Stained or lacquered beech.
H 14½", W 18¼", D 18¼" (37 x 46 x 46 cm)
Producer: Iform

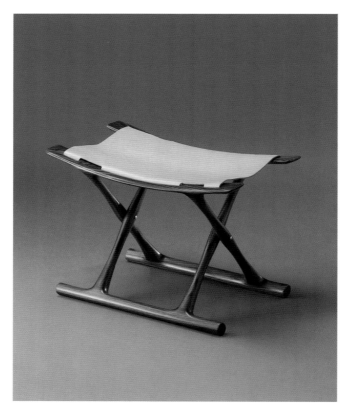

2-272

2-272
#PJ-2000 Egyptian Stool
Design: Ole Wanscher, 1960
Leather seat on oak or mahogany.
H 18", W 24", D 15" (46 x 61 x 38 cm)
Producer: P. J. Furniture

2-273
Stool
Design: Bernt, 1956
Maple, ash, or mahogany with woven cane.
Producer: C. N. Jørgensens

2-273

CONTEMPORARY SCANDINAVIAN FURNITURE

2-274
EJ 144
Design: Anne-Mette Jensen and
Morten Ernst, 2001
Leather or fabric upholstered seat,
chrome-plated or black-lacquered
steel legs.
H 17¾", W 43" (45 x 109 cm)
Producer: Erik Jørgensen

2-275
#1063 Stool
Design: Josef Frank, 1941
Leather and cherry wood.
H 13¾", W 20½", D 16½"
(35 x 52 x 42 cm)
Producer: Svenskt Tenn

2-274

2-275

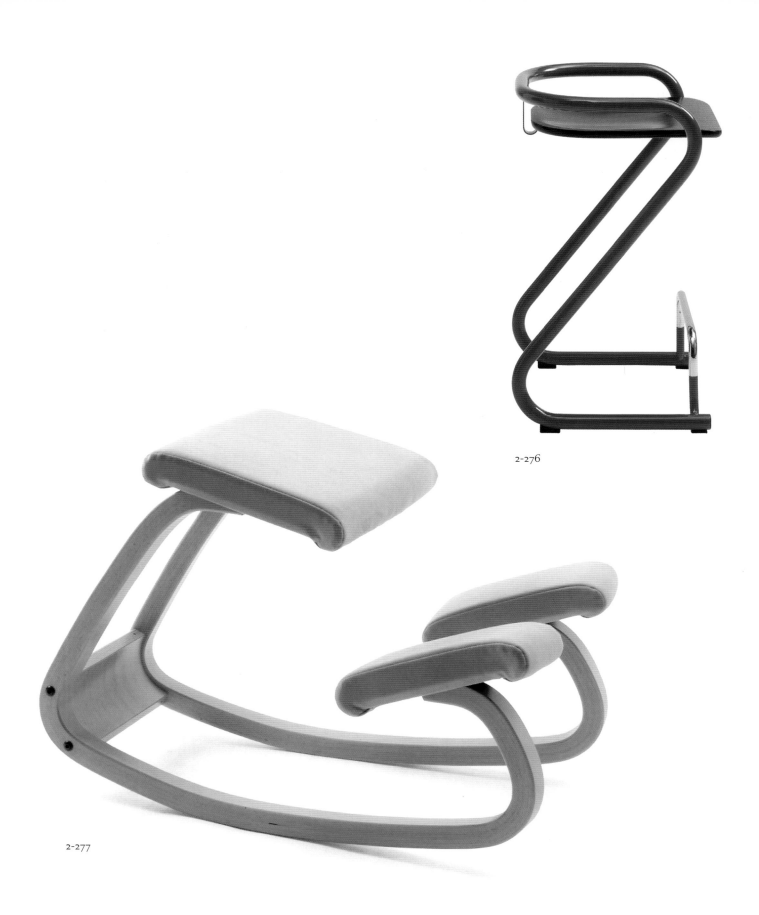

2-276

2-277

Opposite
2-276
S 70 Barstool
Design: Börge Lindau and Bo Lindecrantz, 1968
Natural birch, black, white, or fabric-upholstered seat, chrome-plated or pow-der-coated steel frame; stackable.
H 28", W 19", D 19" (71 x 48 x 48 cm)
Producer: Lammhults

2-277
Balans Variable
Design: Peter Opsvik, 1985
Fabric over foam, laminated beech; avail-able in many versions.
H 20½", W 28½", D 19¾" (52 x 72 x 50 cm)
Producer: Variér

This page
2-278
#4568 Buss Stool
Design: Anna von Schewen
Laminated beech or birch wood, natural or stained; also available as bench.
H 16½", W 16½", D 16½" (42 x 42 x 42 cm)
Producer: Gärsnäs

2-279
#6035 Balans
Design: Peter Opsvik, original 1979
Upholstery over foam, steel base, metal casters; available in many versions.
H 17¼", W 22¾", D 12" (44 x 58 x 30 cm)
Producer: Håg

2-278

2-279

2-280
Robertsfors
Design: Åke Axelsson
Solid oak slats on cast-iron frame.
Producer: Gärsnäs

2-281
Twister
Design: Yuriko Takahashi
Right- and left-sided stools, laminated
birch veneer or black-stained frame,
linked with chrome-plated steel brackets.
H 17¾", W 16¼", D 16¼" (45 x 41 x 41 cm)
Producer: Swedese

2-280

2-281

2-282
Joy Bench
Design: Nanna Ditzel, 1999
Solid maple.
H 18½", W 48, 56, or 71¾", D 18½"
(47 x 122, 142, or 182 x 47 cm)
Producer: Getama (Photo: Erik Brahl)

2-283
Mojo Platform
Design: Hans Thyge Raunkjaer, 2002
Fabric upholstery over wood frame, foam and
pocket springs, brushed aluminum legs; available
in many colors, oval or "sunglass" shape.
Oval: H 14", W 55", D 23½" (36 x 140 x 60 cm)
Sunglass: H 14", W 58¼", D 23" (36 x 149 x 59 cm)
Producer: Stouby

2-282

2-283

2-284

2-284
SA-310 Boomerang
Design: Alexander Lervik, 2004
Laminated birch frame, chrome-plated
tubular steel base.
H 17¾", W 114½", D 56¾" (45 x 291 x 144 cm)
Producer: Skandiform

2-285
#9503 Space Bench
Design: Flemming Busk + Stephan B.
Hertzog, 2003
Fabric upholstery over foam, birch and steel
frame; available also as single elements, with
or without attached tables.
H 21¾", W 122", D 141" (55 x 310 x 358 cm)
Producer: Magnus Olesen

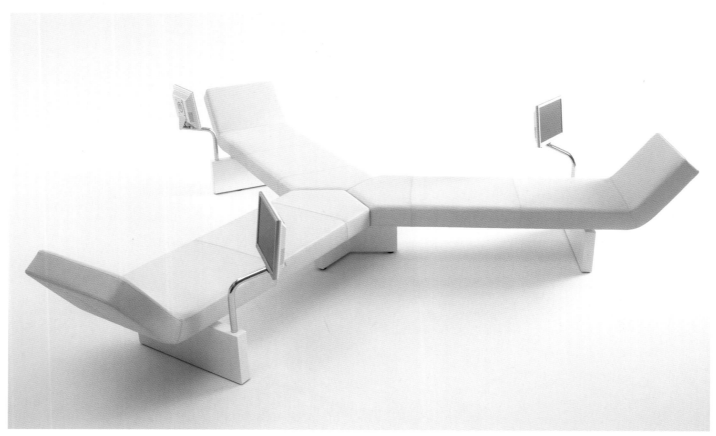

2-285

2-286
Bank
Design: Love Arbén, 1997
Upholstery over cold-processed polyester
foam, molded birch seat, powder-coated
steel frame.
H 43", W 78¾", D 17" (109 x 200 x 43 cm)
Producer: Lammhults

2-286

2-287
Ice
Design: Kasper Salto, 2002
Molded synthetic material on aluminum
base, optional upholstered seat; available
in six colors, also with arms, in counter
or barstool height. Suitable indoors or
outdoors.
H 38¼ or 43", W 22", D 21"
(97 or 109 x 56 x 53 cm)
Producer: Fritz Hansen

2-288

2-288
Cobra
Design: Mattias Ljunggren, 1990
Oak, natural or stained birch, fabric,
or leather seat on angled stainless steel
frame.
H 17¾, 25½, or 33½"; W 8½", D 12½"
(45, 65, or 85 x 22 x 32 cm)
Producer: Källemo

2-287

2-289
S-045 Afternoon
Design: Eero Koivisto, 2004
Laminated birch, chrome-plated tubular
steel base.
H 36½", W 19¼", D 14" (93 x 49 x 35 cm)
Producer: Skandiform

2-290
Trinidad
Design: Nanna Ditzel, 1993
Maple, cherry, beech, birch, or walnut fan-
shaped fretwork back and seat, tubular
steel frame; also available in black or white
lacquer .
H 44¼", W 17¾", D 19¾" (112 x 45 x 50 cm)
Producer: Fredericia

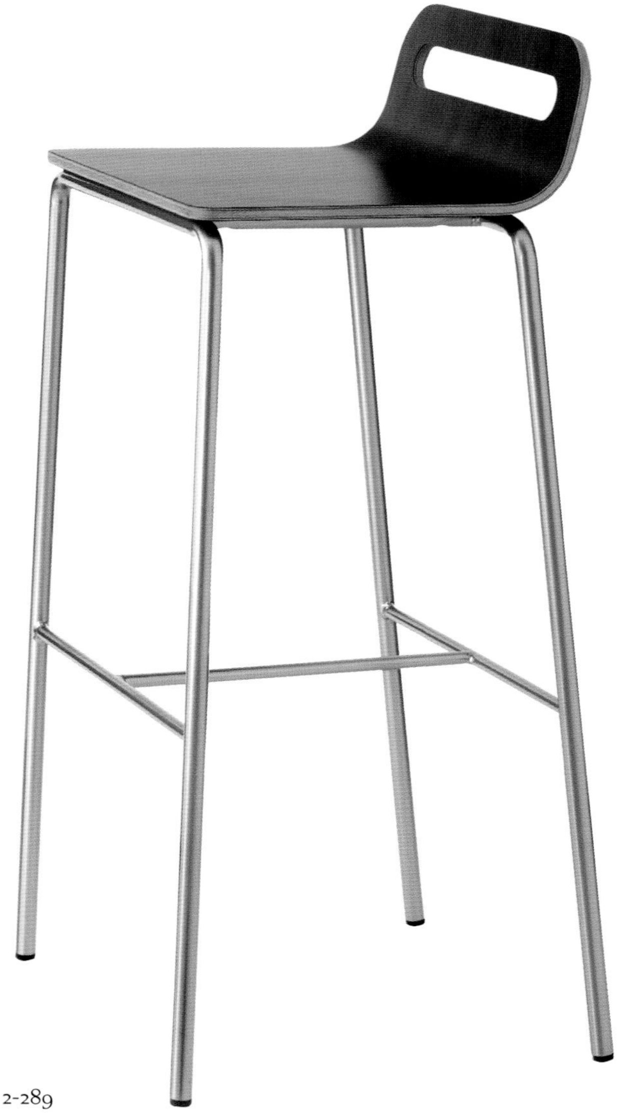

2-289

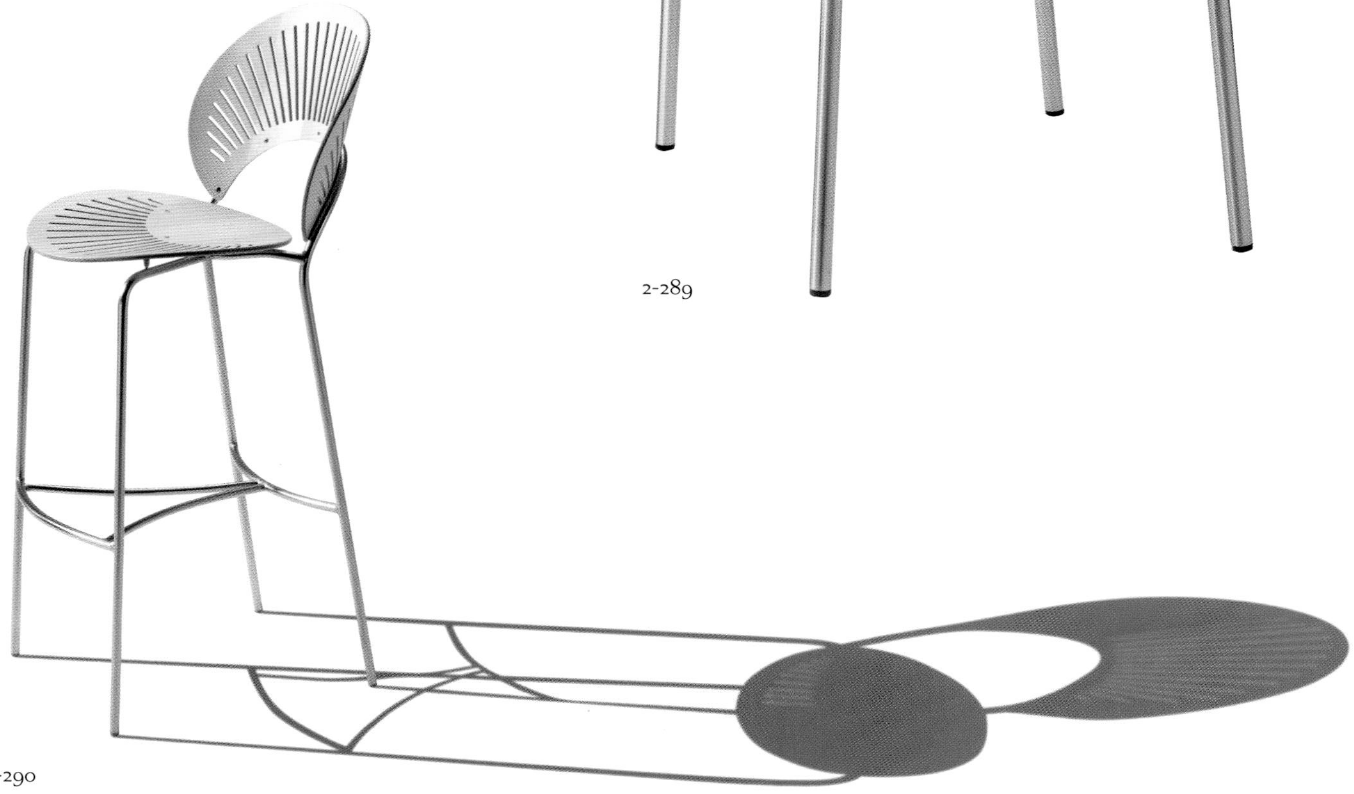

2-290

2-291

2-291
Move
Design: Per Øie, 1986
Rocking stool, upholstery over steel,
adjustable height
H 19¼– 26¾", 22–32¼" or 25½–34¼"
(49–68, 56–82, or 65– 87 cm)
Producer: Variér

2-292
Vera Stool
Design: Teemu Järvi, 2005
Form-pressed plywood seat, natural or
stained birch, oak, or ash, or upholstered,
on steel rod frame; available in three
heights, stackable.
Producer: HKT Korhonen

2-292

2-293

2-293
Bench for Two
Design: Nanna Ditzel, 1989
Curve-back bench of aircraft plywood
laminated in striped pattern, sycamore,
chrome/matte chrome, silver; companion
table available.
H 38½", W 59", D 27½"
(98 x 150 x 70 cm)
Producer: Fredericia

2-294
Astral
Design: Per Borre, 1979
Matchstick slat bench, ash, sycamore, or
oiled teak; available as two elements form-
ing a semicircle; for indoor or outdoor use.
H 32½", W 52", D 27½"
(83 x 133 x 70 cm)
Producer: Fredericia

2-294

DINING TABLES

2-295

2-296

Previous page
2-295
PK-54A
Design: Poul Kjærholm, 1963
Marble top, solid maple six-piece interlocking
extension ring, stainless steel base. (Seats 12;
without extensions, seats 6.)
H 27¼", Diam. 82¾" (69, 210 cm)
Producer: Fritz Hansen

2-296
Extension Table H92
Design: Alvar Aalto, 1936 and 1956
Natural lacquered birch, ash veneer top.
H 28½, 23½, or 20½", L 51¼", W 35½"; two
19¾" leaves
(72, 60, or 52 x 130 x 90; 50+50 cm)
Producer: Artek

2-297
Table 81B
Design: Alvar Aalto, 1933–35
Natural birch, birch or ash veneer, lino-
leum or laminate top; also available as
coffee table.
H 28½", L 47¼", D 29½"
(72 x 120 x 75 cm)
Producer: Artek

2-298
Table 95
Design: Aino and Alvar Aalto, 1933–35
Lacquered natural birch, birch or ash
veneer, linoleum or laminate top; also
available as coffee table.
H 28½", Diam. 47¼" (72, 120 cm)
Producer: Artek

2-297

2-298

2-299

2-299
B412 Superellipse
Design: Piet Hein and Bruno Matthson, 1968
Walnut top, chrome-plated metal spanlegs; available in three heights.
H 28½, 27, or 20½", L 59", D 39¼" (72, 70, or 52 x 150 x 100 cm)
Producer: Fritz Hansen

2-300
2K
Design: Tony Almén and Peter Gest
Red laminate top, oak frame.
H 28¼", L 47¼", WD 47¼" (72 x 120 x
120cm)
Producer: Karl Andersson

2-301
Triptyk
Design: Jonas Bohlin, 1998
Solid ash or laminated board/ash top,
black cast-iron base; available as small
cast-iron table.
H 28½", L 82¾", D 27½" (72 x 210 x 70 cm)
Producer: Källemo

2-300

2-301

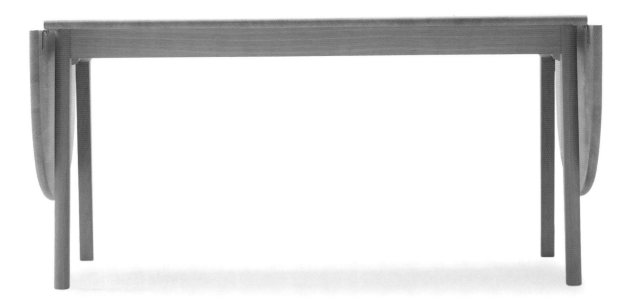

2-302

2-303

2-302
CH 006 Drop-leaf Table
Design: Hans J. Wegner, 1982
Beech or oak.
H 28½", L 54¼", D 28½" (+ two 19¼" leaves)
(72 x 138 x 72+49+49 cm)
Producer: Carl Hansen (Photo: Søren Larson)

2-303
#219 Square-legged Table
Design: Knud Andersen, 2003
Beech, oak, maple, ash, walnut, American or European cherry, or
walnut; available in five lengths and four widths.
H 28", L 63–94½", W 37½–43¼" (74 x 160–240 x 95–110 cm)
Producer: Brdr-Andersen

2-304
#281 Pedestal Base Dining Table
Design: Knud Andersen, 1980
Beech, oak, or ash; available in three sizes.
H 28", L 57, 75, or 94"; D 37"
(71 x 145, 190, or 240 x 95 cm)
Producer: Brdr-Andersen

2-305
#263 Rounded-end Dining Table
Design: Knud Andersen, 1998
Beech, oak, maple, ash, cherry, or walnut.
H 27½", L 55", D 35 or L 63", D 39"
(70 x 139 x 89 or 70 x 160 x 99 cm)
Producer: Brdr-Andersen

2-306
#208 Gate-leg Table
Design: Hans J. Wegner, 1975
Beech, maple, oak, or cherry.
H 27½", L 35½", W 26¾" (+ two 24" leaves)
(70 x 90 x 68+62+62 cm)
Producer: Getama
(Photo: Erik Brahl)

2-304

2-305

2-306

2-307

2-308

2-307
CH 327
Design: Hans J. Wegner, 1962
Maple, ash, beech, oak, cherry, or walnut.
H 28½", L 74¾ or 97¾, W 37¼ (72 x 190 or 248 x 95 cm)
Producer: Carl Hansen (Photo: Søren Larson)

2-308
CH 318
Design: Hans J. Wegner, 1960
Maple, ash, beech, oak, cherry, or walnut top; steel base and legs.
H 28½", L 63, 75, or 95", D 37½" (72 x 160, 190, or 240 x 95 cm)
Producer: Carl Hansen (Photo: Søren Larson)

2-309
Atelier Table
Design: Niels Jørgen Haugesen, 1980s
Sycamore top and trestle legs, stainless
steel supports.
H 28", L 75 or 95", D 37"
(71 x 190½ or 241 x 94 cm)
Producer: Axelsen
(not in current production)

2-310
Collapsible Table
Design: Niels Jørgen Haugesen, 1984
Ash top, steel base, fold-out side
extensions.
H 27½", L 75"–120", D 36"
(70 x 190 or 305 x 91 cm)
Producer: Fredericia

2-309

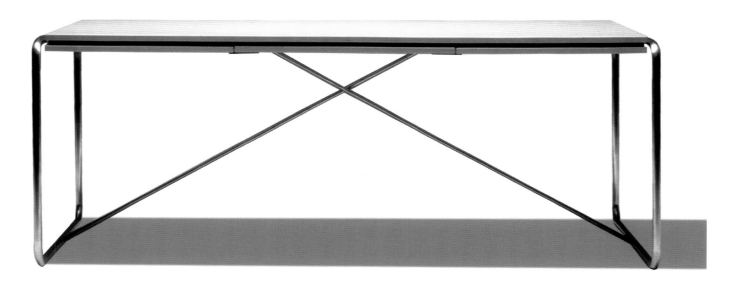

2-310a

2-310b

2-3II

2-3II
Menu Table
Design: Strand & Hvass
Solid ash; adjustable leg allows for three or
four chairs along sides.
L 102¼" (260 cm)
Producer: Fredericia

2-312
#3850
Design: Bernt, 2003
Beech or maple top, tubular chrome-
plated steel legs or wood legs; extension
available.
H 28½", L 63", D 47¼"
(72 x 160 x 120 cm)
Producer: Getama (Photo: Erik Brahl)

2-312

2-313

2-313
PP 75
Design: Hans J. Wegner, 1982
Clear-lacquered oak or ash, metal
cross-struts.
H 27½", Diam. 55" (70, 140 cm)
Producer: PP Møbler

2-314
#947 Extension Table
Design: Josef Frank
Pyramid mahogany with narrow intarsia,
supporting legs.
H 28½", L 59–153", D 43," (+ four 23½"
leaves)
(72 x 150–390 x 110 cm, leaves 60 cm)
Producer: Svenskt Tenn

2-314a

2-314b

2-315

2-315
Trippo
Design: Ulla Christiansson, 2006
Table system. Round, square, rectangular, or oval wood or laminate
tops, chrome-plated steel legs, available in six heights and forty-two
combinations of shapes and sizes.
H 11¾–28¼", L 27½–94½", D 15¾–24¾" (30–72 x 70–240 x 40–63 cm)
Producer: Karl Andersson

COFFEE & OCCASIONAL TABLES

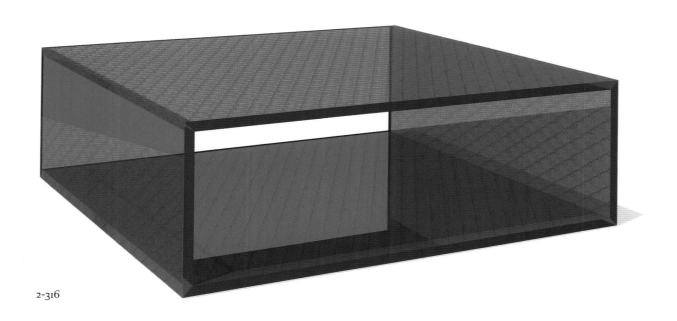

2-316

Previous page
2-316
Cell
Design: Eero Koivisto, 2005
Orange or glass-green acrylic.
H 12, 19¾, or 39¼" square
(30, 50, or 100 cm square)
Producer: Offecct
(Photo: Peter Fotograf)

This page
2-317
Design: Nissen & Gehl
Ash, walnut, oak, beech or cherry, stain-
less steel legs, with or without glass shelf.
Also available in smaller oval, round or
square shapes.
H 18", L 66½", D 19¾" (45 x 170 x 50 cm)
Producer: Aksel Kjersgaard

2-317

2-318

2-318
EJ 65-6
Design: Johannes Foersom and Peter
Hiort-Lorenzen, 1999
Oak or granite table top, matte satin
finish, chrome-plated steel legs.
H 15", L 31½", D 31½" or L 17¾", D 51¼"
(38 x 80 x 80 or 38 x 45 x 130 cm)
Producer: Erik Jørgensen

2-319
Vertigo
Design: Eero Koivisto, 2005
Glass top, mirror base, chrome-plated
metal frame.
H 15¾", L 35½", W 35½" (40 x 90 x 90 cm)
Producer: Offecct (Photo: Peter Fotograf)

2-320
PK-61
Design: Poul Kjærholm, 1955
Plate glass top, stainless steel base.
H 12½", L 31½", D 31½" (32 x 80 x 80 cm)
Producer: Fritz Hansen

2-319

2-320

2-321

2-322

Opposite
2-321
O Table
Design: Heikki Ruoho, 2004
Veneered tabletop, polished or matte chrome-plated steel pedestal,
veneered plywood base; available in three heights, with round, square,
or rectangular tops in several sizes.
H 21¼, 28, or 43", Tops 23½" round or square to 39" x 86" rectangular
(55, 71, or 109 cm, tops 60 x 60 to 100 x 220 cm)
Producer: HKT Korhonen

2-322
PK-71
Design: Poul Kjærholm, 1957
Nesting square-top tables, acrylic and stainless steel.
Nested: H 29", L 29", D 29" (74 x 74 x 74 cm)
Producer: Fritz Hansen

2-323

2-323
Tray
Design: Monica Förster, 2004
Natural or lacquered wood tabletops, chrome-plated metal base;
underside of tray polyurethane anti-glide surface.
H 21", Diam. 19¾ (53, 50 cm)
Producer: Offecct (Photo: Peter Fotograf)

2-324
Concrete
Design: Jonas Bohlin, 1984
Plate glass top, concrete base,
steel frame.
H 21¼ or 28¼", L 60", D 10–30"
(54 or 72 x 150 x 25–75 cm)
Producer: Källemo

2-325
København
Design: Michael Poulsen
and Hans Ploug, 2005
Glass top, oak base.
H 18", L 31½", D 31½" (46 x 80 x 80 cm)
Producer: Karl Andersson

2-324

2-325

2-326

2-326
Scimitar
Design: Preben Fabricius and Jørgen
Kastholm, 1965
Glass top, tubular steel frame.
H 17", Diam. 47¼" (43, 119 cm)
Producer: Bo-Ex

2-327

2-327
Hockney Coffee Table
Design: Eero Koivisto, 1999
Lacquered white or anthracite top, steel base.
H 12", L 47¼", W 31½", or 31½" square (30 x 120 x 80 or 30 x 80 x 80 cm)
Producer: David Design

2-328
Spider
Design: Andreas Hansen, 1990
Table system. Plate glass top, tubular steel base; available with round or square top in several sizes and as dining table.
Coffee table: H 15½"–17¾" (39–45 cm)
Dining table: H 28"–30¼" (71–77 cm)
Producer: Eilersen

2-329
Mirror
Design: Nanna Ditzel
Glass top, stainless steel base.
H 17¼", Diam. 50" (44, 127 cm)
Producer: Fredericia

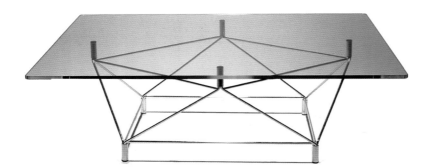

2-328

2-329

2-330

2-330
Lotus Table
Design: Flemming Busk + Stephan B. Hertzog
Hardened frosted, pale frosted, or colored glass, walnut veneer,
black or white laminate, or linoleum top, tubular metal legs.
H 15", Diam. 35" (38, 90 cm)
Producer: Globe

2-331

2-331
#907C Double Coffee Table
Design: Alvar Aalto, 1933
Lacquered natural or honey-tone birch,
birch or ash veneer top; available in several
variations. Companion stools.
H 22", Diam. 23½" (56, 60 cm)
Producer: Artek

2-332
Sven
Design: Mats Theselius, 1999
Birch top, matte chrome or coppered steel
frame.
Producer: Källemo

2-332

2-333
Bedside Table
Design: Morten Brorsen, 2002
Wood veneer over aluminum core; coordinated with flexible
storage modules.
Producer: GUBI-Cinal Collection

2-334
Coffee Table
Design: Morten Brorsen, 2002
Wood veneer, several finishes, over aluminum core; coordinated
with flexible storage modules.
Producer: GUBI-Cinal Collection

2-333

2-334

2-335

2-335
CH 008
Design: Hans J. Wegner, 1954
Maple, beech, oak, or walnut.
Available in several sizes.
H 17¼, 19, or 20¾", Diam. 30¾, 34¾, 39¼,
or 47¼"
(44, 48, or 53 x 78, 88, 100, 120 cm)
Producer: Carl Hansen
(Photo: Søren Larson)

2-336
Mondial Coffee Table
Design: Nanna Ditzel, 2000
Ash, walnut, or oak.
H 19", Diam. 39¼" +14" extensions
(48, 100 + 36 cm)
Producer: Getama (Photo: Erik Brahl)

2-336

2-337
Dual
Design: Eero Koivisto, 2002
Wood veneer or white lacquer MDF
top, chrome-plated or silver-lacquered metal legs.
H 12", 47¼" square or W 31½" x D 47¼"
(32 x 120 x 120 or 12 x 80 x 120 cm)
Producer: Offecct (Photo: Peter Fotograf)

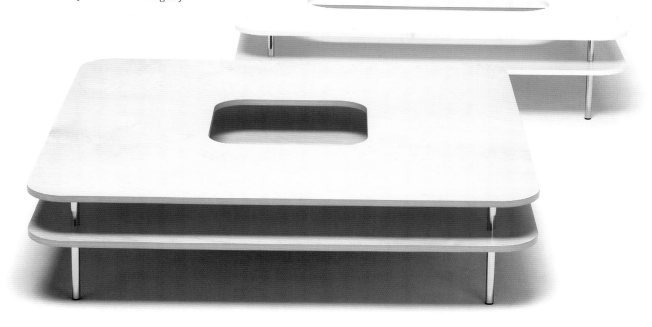

2-337

2-338

2-338
Clips
Design: Jens Juul Eilersen, 2001
Lacquered walnut, oak, or maple, oiled cherry, natural or
black-stained or oiled mahogany veneers; on casters.
H 11¾", 39¼" or 49¼" square (30 x 100 or 125 cm)
Producer: Eilersen

2-339
Wheeler
Design: Jouni Leino, 2001
MDF top, epoxy-coated steel base, casters.
H 28", L 25¼", D 17" (71 x 64 x 43 cm)
Producer: Inno

2-340
Neptune
Design: Alexander Lervik
White or black molded plastic.
Producer: Johanson Design

2-341
Anika
Design: Anika Reuterswärd
Set of nested tables, cherry or oak, with
glass or wood tops.
H 17", W 40 or 35", L 35" (45 x 40 x 35 cm)
Producer: Fogia

2-339

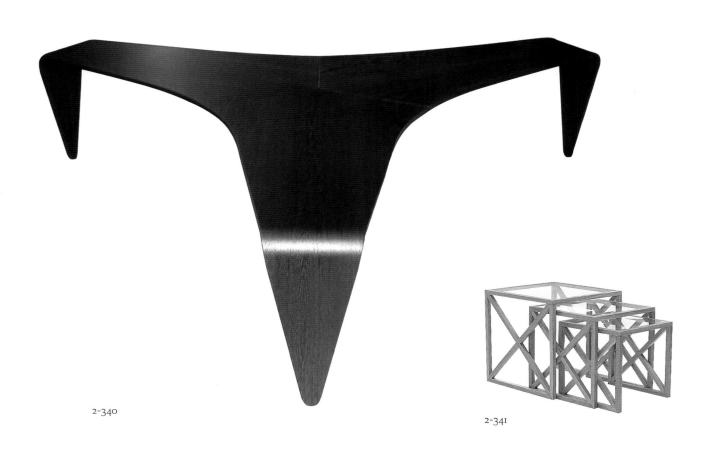

2-340

2-341

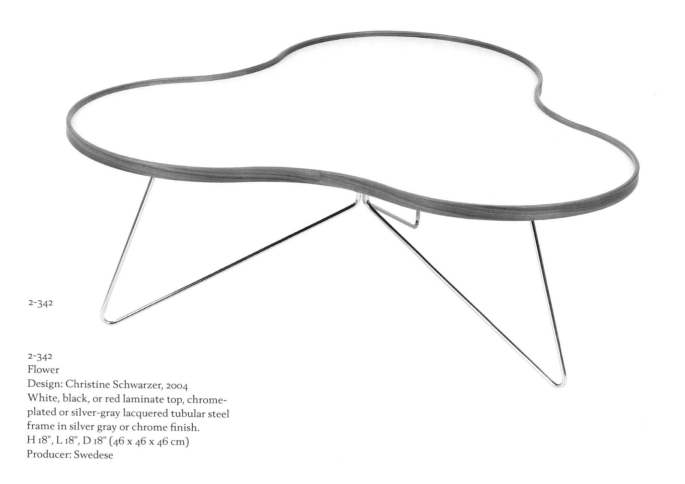

2-342

2-342
Flower
Design: Christine Schwarzer, 2004
White, black, or red laminate top, chrome-plated or silver-gray lacquered tubular steel frame in silver gray or chrome finish.
H 18", L 18", D 18" (46 x 46 x 46 cm)
Producer: Swedese

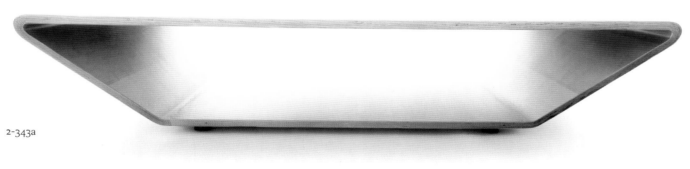

2-343a

2-343
Brasilia
Design: Ola Rune and Eero Koivisto, 2002
Laminated birch, oak, or walnut.
H 28", 39¼" or 47¼" square
(71 x 100 or 120 x 120 cm)
Producer: Swedese

2-343b

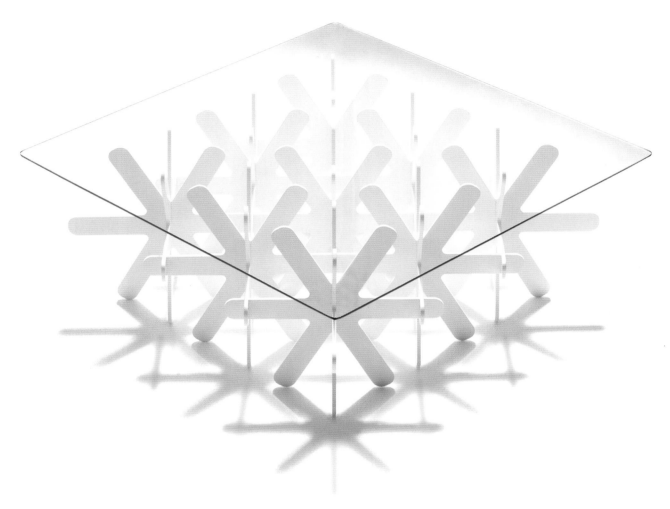

2-344

2-344
Snow
Design: Nendo, 2005
Safety glass top, white-lacquered, veneer-coated MDF "snowflake."
base, available in two sizes.
H 12", L 49", W 27½", D 27½" or H 12", L 29", D 27½"
(30 x 125 x 70 or 30 x 70 x 70 cm)
Producer: Swedese

2-345
B404
Design: Piet Hein and Bruno Matthsson,
1968
White synthetic laminate top, chrome-
plated steel legs; available in three heights.
H 20½", 27½", or 28½", Diam. 45¼"
(52, 70, or 72, Diam. 115 cm)
Producer: Fritz Hansen

2-346
82/85 Coffee Table with Leaves
Design: Hans J. Wegner, 1980
Beech, cherry, or oak; semi-circular leaves.
H 22½", L 37¾", W 29½" (+ two 12½"
leaves) (57 x 96 x 75+32+32 cm)
Producer: Getama (Photo: Erik Brahl)

2-345

2-346

2-347

2-347
Trippo
Design: Ulla Christiansson, 2006
Accessory tables, wood or laminate tops,
chrome-plated steel legs, available in six
heights and seven sizes of top, also oval,
rectangular, or square.
H 21¾", Diam. 23 ¾"; H 15¾", Diam. 17¾"
(53 x Diam. 60; 40 x Diam. 45 cm)
Producer: Karl Andersson

2-348
Tema
Design: Hans Johansson, 2006
Sofa table, glass top on birch base
H 21 ¾", Diam 32" (55, 81.5 cm)
Producer: Karl Andersson

Opposite
2-349
Ovalette
Design: Ilmari Tapiovaara, 1954
Oiled teak or walnut veneer top, patinated
natural birch, black, or oiled walnut base.
H 16 ¾", L 47¼", D 23½" (42.5 x 120 x 60
cm)
Producer: Aero

2-348

STORAGE, SHELVES, & ROOM DIVIDERS

2-351

2-351
City Bureau
Design: Rud Thygesen and Johnny
Sørensen
Maple, cherry, beech, or mahogany units,
wall-mounted or set on plinth base or
casters. Wood or PUR rubber handles,
available with PUR rubber fronts and
sides.
H 15, 29¼, or 71¼", L 13½" or 25¾",
D 13½"or 17¼"
(38, 74, 181 x 34, 65 x 34, 44 cm)
Producer: Eric Boisens
(Photo: Schnakenburg & Brahl)

Previous page
2-350
1300 Sideboard
Design: Nissen & Gehl
Oval silhouette with tambour doors, usable as room
divider. Ash, walnut, oak, beech or cherry, stainless
steel hardware and legs.
H 30¾", L 78¾", D 21" (78 x 200 x 53 cm)
Producer: Aksel Kjersgaard

2-352
#715 Wall-mounted Storage
Cabinet
Design: Ditlev Karsten, 2002
Beech, oak, maple, ash, American
or European cherry, or walnut.
H 20", L 78¾", D 15"
(51 x 200 x 38 cm)
Producer: Brdr-Andersen

2-353
712 Sideboard
Design: Ditlev Karsten, 2002
Beech, oak, maple, ash, American
or European cherry, or walnut.
H 37", L 78¾", D 19½"
(94 x 200 x 38 cm)
Producer: Brdr-Andersen

2-352

2-353

2-354

2-355

2-354
Sundre
Design: Kristian Eriksson, 2004
Modular chest. Birch or oak, limestone
or granite top; available in several heights
and widths.
H 17" to 45½", W 12½" to 71½", D 17 ¾"
(44–116 x 32–182 x 45 cm)
Producer: G.A.D.

2-355
#461 MUP Modular Storage
Design: Pirkko Stenros, 1999
Stacking units, matte white, white with
birch top, white with birch front, all birch,
or all glossy white.
H 32½", L 15¼", D 15¼" (82.5 x 39 x 39 cm)
Producer: Muurame

2-356
Øresund Cabinet
Design: Børge Mogensen, 1955
Pine and teak.
H 33", L 80", D 18" (84 x 203 x 46 cm)
Producer: Karl Andersson

2-356

2-357
#420 Classic Moduli Chest of Drawers
Design: Pirkko Stenros, 1955
Modular units; available all matte white,
white with birch top, white with birch
front, all birch, or all glossy white.
H 14½", L 20½", D 20½" (37 x 52 x 52 cm)
Producer: Muurame

2-358
2K
Design: Tony Almén and Peter Gest, 2000
Oak, natural or red finish, glass doors.
H 81", L 35½", D 14¼" (206 x 90 x 36 cm)
Producer: Karl Andersson

2-357

2-358

2-359

2-359
Centro
Kenneth Wikström, 2000
Plywood cabinet
Dimensions:
Producer: Formverk

2-360a

2-360
Moka Sideboard
Design: Moni Beuchel, 2003
Oak and wenge wood, wood doors; also
available with glass doors, round legs.
H 20¼", L 59¾", D 15" (51 x 150 x 38 cm)
Producer: Karl Andersson

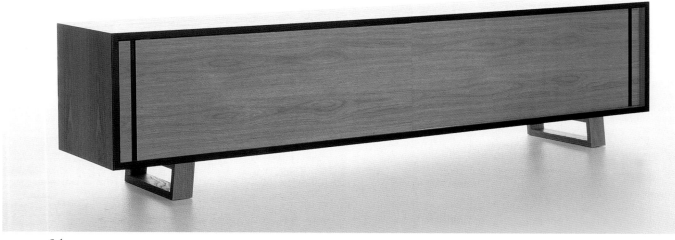

2-360b

2-361

2-361
2077 Vitrine
Design: Josef Frank, 1946
Light mahogany frame, glass sides.
H 66½", L 35½", D 31" (169 x 90 x 78 cm)
Producer: Svenskt Tenn

2-362
Ono
Design: Love Arbén, 1992
Maple veneer plywood, white and black laminate stripes,
enameled gray steel base.
H 53¼", L 19¾", D 19¾" (135 x 50 x 50 cm)
Producer: Lammhults

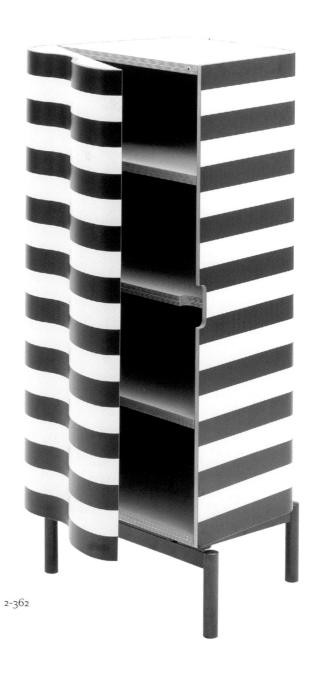

2-362

2-363

2-363
#1270 China Cabinet
Design: Nissen & Gehl
Ash, walnut, oak, beech, or cherry, glass
doors, stainless steel base.
H 66½", L 47½", D 19" (170 x 120 x 48 cm)
Producer: Aksel Kjersgaard

2-364

2-364
Bookcase-system
Design: Mogens Koch, 1928
Stacking bookshelf units in pine, Oregon pine, oak,
mahogany, ash, European cherry, or teak.
Each unit: H 30", L 30", D 10¾" or 14" (76 x 76 x 27, 36 cm)
Producer: Rud. Rasmussen

2-365
#881 Chest of Drawers
Design: Josef Frank, late 1930s
Wovona root and walnut, various-sized drawers, brass pulls.
H 47¼", W 35½", D 17¾" (120 x 90 x 45 cm)
Producer: Svenskt Tenn

2-366
Funk
Design: Per Söderberg, 2000
Painted MDF with birch, oak, or aluminum, sliding or hinged doors,
anodized aluminum legs; available in several heights and widths.
H 16¼", 30¼", 44½", 58¾"; L 32¼", 62½", 93"; D 17¾"
(41, 77, 113, 149 x 82, 159, 236 x 45 cm)
Producer: David Design

2-365

2-366

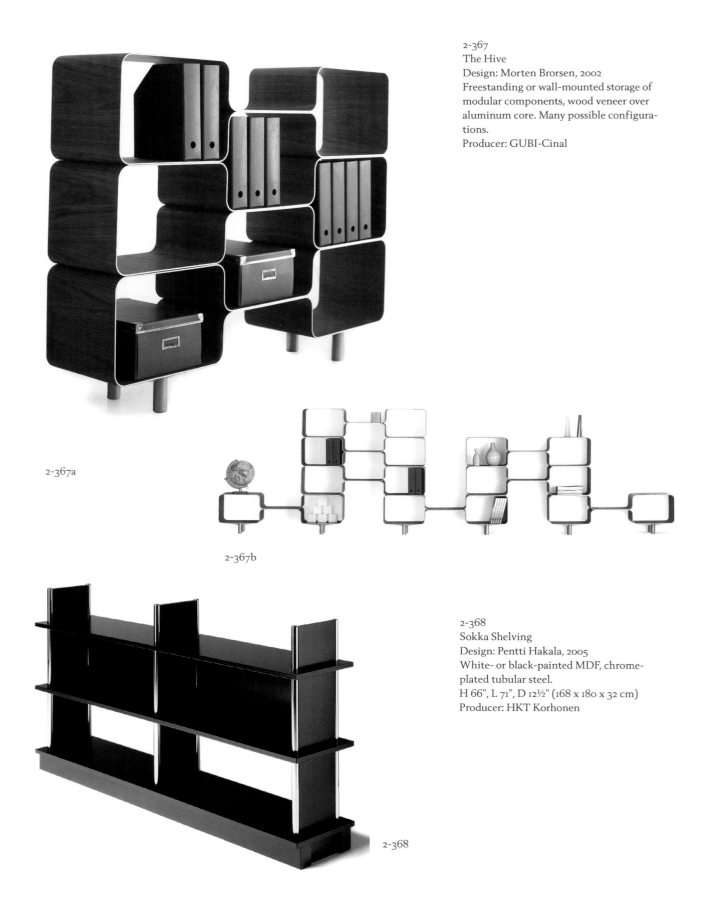

2-367
The Hive
Design: Morten Brorsen, 2002
Freestanding or wall-mounted storage of modular components, wood veneer over aluminum core. Many possible configurations.
Producer: GUBI-Cinal

2-367a

2-367b

2-368
Sokka Shelving
Design: Pentti Hakala, 2005
White- or black-painted MDF, chrome-plated tubular steel.
H 66", L 71", D 12½" (168 x 180 x 32 cm)
Producer: HKT Korhonen

2-368

2-369

2-369
Raami Play
Design: Rauno Sorsa, 2005
Black, white, or natural lacquered modular
units, painted or veneered MDF; available
open or with doors or drawers.
H 14", L 19½", D 14" (36 x 50 x 36 cm)
Producer: HKT Korhonen

2-370
Vilter Works Shelving
Design: Yrjö Wiherheimo, 2006
Shelf unit on casters, square steel tubing
frame, solid laminate shelves.
Coordinated desk and auxiliary tables
available.
Producer: Vivero

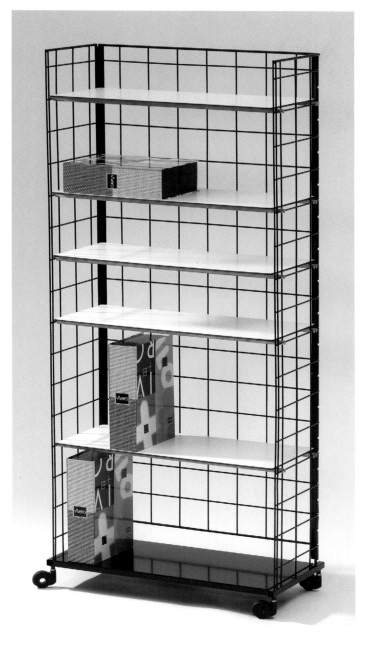

2-370

2-371
Skyline
Design: Sigurdur Gustafsson, 1998
Shelves with aluminum surface, stained MDF.
H 27½", L 81", D 26¾" (70 x 206 x 68 cm)
Producer: Källemo

2-372
Bonsai Storage Units
Design: Ditlev Karsten, 2004
Beech, oak, maple, ash, American or European cherry, or walnut; glass fronts, plinth or leg-plinth base; available in many sizes.
H 12"–73", W 24"–71¼", D 12"–20"
(30–188 x 61–181 x 30–51 cm)
Producer: Brdr-Andersen

2-371

2-372

2-373
Shelf Storage
Design: EB
Modular system. Beech, birch, or painted gray frame, beech or birch shelves.
Producer: Erik Boisens

2-374
#451 Super Neppari
Design: Pirkko Stenros, 1975
Modular units. All matte white, white with birch top, white with birch front, all birch, or all glossy white.
H 32½", L 20½", D 10¼ (82 x 52 x 26 cm)
Producer: Muurame

2-373

2-374

2-376

2-375

2-375
Montana
Design: Peter J. Lassen, 1982
Modular system. Forty-two basic units, seven widths and four
depths; available in many colors, veneers, mirrors, and glass.
Producer: Montana

2-376
Kontur
Design: Tony Almén and Peter Gest, 2006
Multi-purpose flexible storage units with many options; available
in: four heights, two widths, and different configurations, including
combinations of doors, glass, or open fronts. Finishes include oak,
black, off-white or special colors.
H 23¾, 32, 46¼, or 77½", W 17¾ or 35¼", D 14¼"
(60, 81.5, 117.7, or 196.7 x 45 or 90 x 36 cm)
Producer: Karl Andersson

2-377

2-377
Trippo
Ulla Christiansson, 2006
Wall-mounted multi-purpose shelf units,
black or yellow lacquer finish.
72½", L 15¼", D 9" (184 x 40 x 23 cm)
Producer: Karl Andersson

2-378
Zigzag
Design: Dögg Gudmundsdöttir, 2005
Flexible modular elements, aluminum;
assemble as bench or shelf units.
As shown: H 68½", L 34½", D 14¼"
(174 x 87 x 36 cm)
Producer: Sólóhusgögn

2-378

MISCELLANEOUS

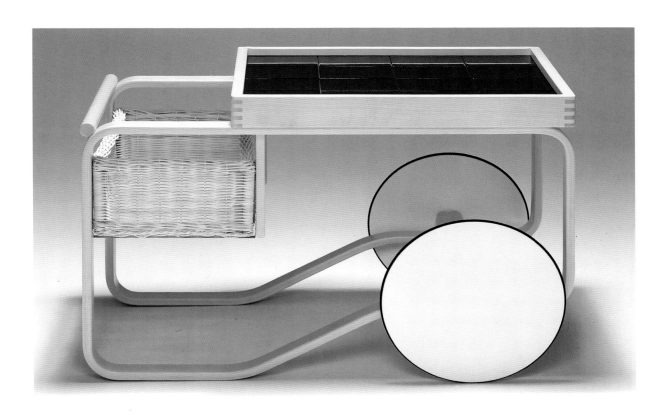

2-379

2-380

Previous page
2-379
Tea Trolley
Design: Alvar Aalto, 1936–37
Natural lacquered birch, white or black
ceramic tiles, rattan basket.
H 23½", L 25½", D 35½" (60 x 65 x 90 cm)
Producer: Artek

This page
2-380
Pick Up
Design: Alfredo Häberli, 2004
Fabric upholstery over cold-cured foam,
flameproof fiber seat and back, wood
frame, metal and rubber wheels.
H 16½", L 24½", D 12" (42 x 62 x 30 cm)
Producer: Offecct
(Photo: Peter Fotograf)

2-381
Planka
Design: Börge Lindau and Bo
Lindecrantz, 1986
Lacquered wood back, perforated sheet
metal seat, leather or fabric cushions.
H 41¾", D 27½" (106 x 70 cm)
Producer: Lammhults

2-381

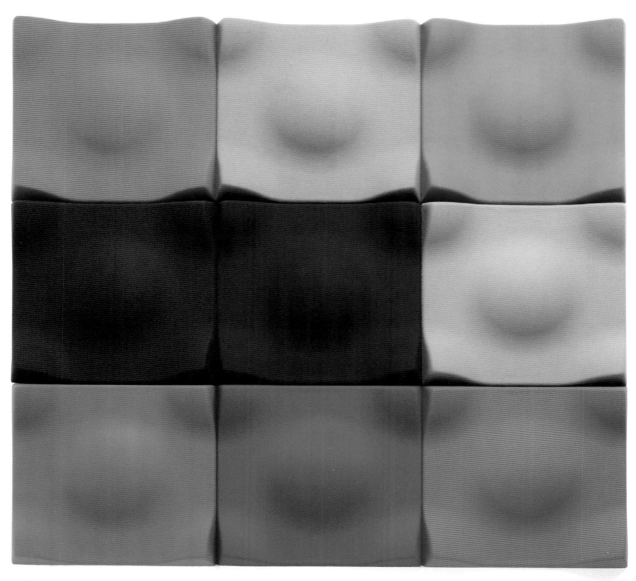

2-382

2-382
Swell Soundwave
Design: Teppo Asikainen, 2004
Decorative acoustical wall panels, molded
polyester fiber.
H 23", W 23", D 3¼" (58.5 x 58.5 x 8 cm)
Producer: Offecct (Photo: Peter Fotograf)

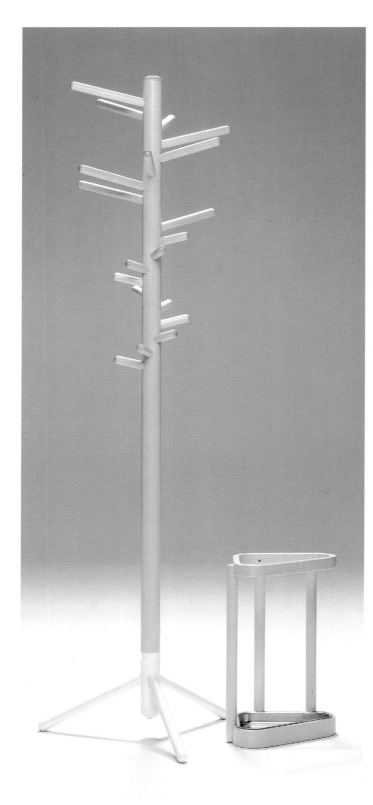

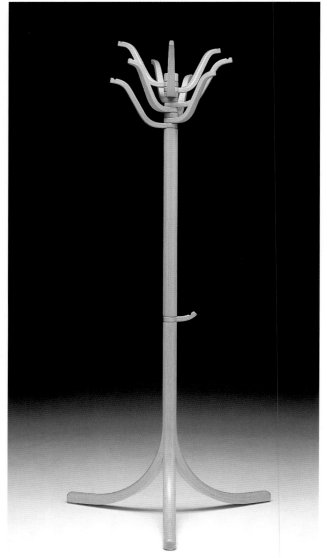

2-384

2-383
#160 Clothes Tree
Design: Anna-Maija Jaatinen, 1960s
Natural lacquered birch, white- or black-lacquered metal foot.
H 69¾", Diam. 24" (177, 61 cm)
Producer: Artek

2-384
#8039 Coat Rack
Design: Rud Thygesen & Johnny Sørensen, 1981
Laminated beech.
H 68", L 29½", D 29½" (173 x 75 x 75 cm)
Producer: Magnus Olesen

2-383

2-385
Tree Coat Hanger
Design: Michael Young and Katrin
Petursdottir, 2002
Birch veneer, white- or black-lacquered;
available also in wall-mounted
version.
H 76½", W 35", D 19¾" (194 x 89 x 50 cm)
Producer: Swedese

2-385

2-386

2-386
Aalto Working Desk
Design: Andreas Engesvik, 2002
Birch, oak, walnut, matte lacquer, or
painted white molded top; matte chrome-
plated steel tubing base.
H 28¼", L 47¼", D 27½" (72 x 120 x 70 cm)
Producer: David Design

2-387
PP 586 Fruit Bowl
Design: Hans J. Wegner, 1956
Ash or oak, steel wire legs.
H 12½", Diam. 25½" (32, 65 cm)
Producer: PP Møbler

2-387

2-388

2-388
Zink
Design: Jonas Bohlin, 1984
Hanging wall shelf, solid birch,
natural or stained in color.
H 13¾", L 61", D 10½" (35 x 155 x 27 cm)
Producer: Källemo

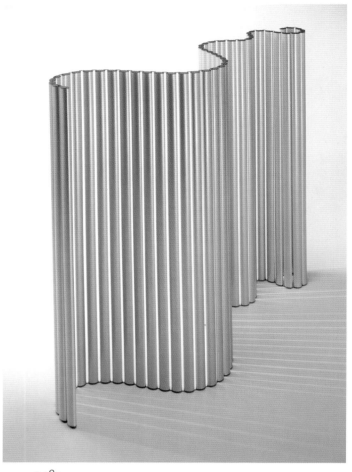

2-389

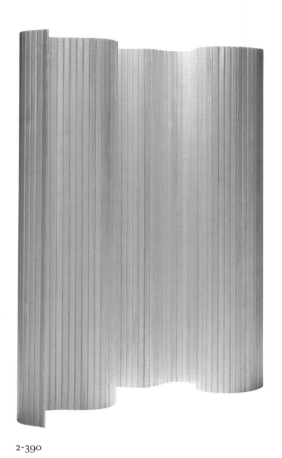

2-390

2-391

2-389
Viper #VC300
Design: Hans Sandgren Jakobsen, 1996
Flexible divider screen, aluminum or
cardboard.
H 63", L 118" (160 x 300 cm)
Producer: Fritz Hansen

2-390
Screen 100
Design: Alvar Aalto, 1933–36
Natural lacquered pine.
H 59½", L 79" (150 x 200 cm)
Producer: Artek

2-391
Curtain-form screen
Front Design, 2005
Flexible plastic, red or white.
H 59¼", W 47¼", D 13¾" (150 x 120 x 35 cm)
Producer: Materia
(Photo: Anna Lönnerstam)

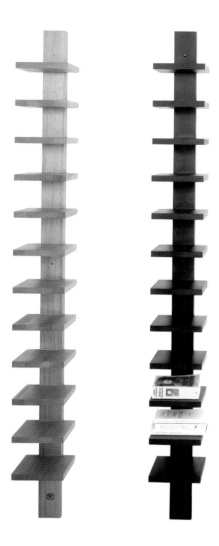

2-392

2-392
Pilaster
Design: John Kandell, 1989
Natural or stained birch or oak.
H 80¾", L 7¾", D 8½" (205 x 20 x 22 cm)
Producer: Källemo

2-393
Collage
Design: Dan Ihreborn, 1992
Flexible shelf-storage system, birch; avail-
able as open or closed shelves, or with cabinet
attachments.
Producer: Kallin & Franzén (Move-range)

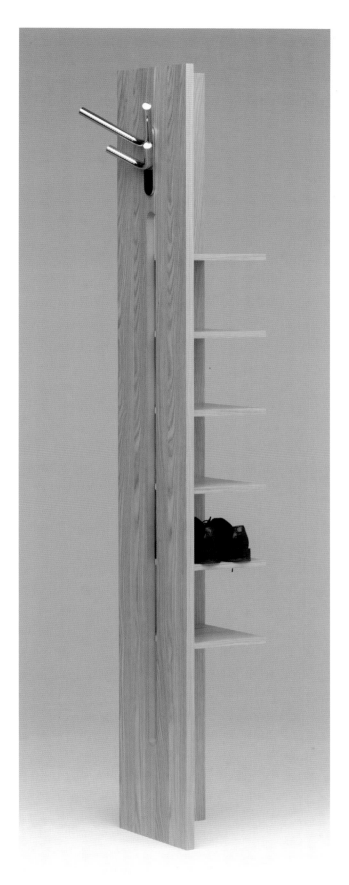

2-393

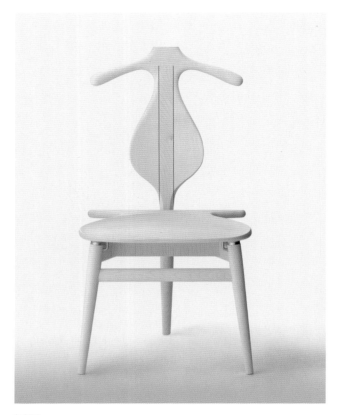

2-394

2-395

2-396

2-394
PP 250 Valet Chair
Design: Hans J. Wegner, 1953
Maple, mahogany, cherry, or teak.
H 37½", L 19¾", D 19¾" (95 x 50 x 50 cm)
Producer: PP Møbler

2-395
Giraffe Stepstool
Design: Chuck Mack, 2005
Nickel-plated steel tubing frame, wood seat and cap, available in a
variety of colors or natural wood veneers.
H 41", Diam. 12" (119, 30 cm)
Producer: Sólóhusgögn

2-396
#616 High Chair
Design: Ben af Schulten, 1965
Natural lacquered birch, birch veneer back, natural or lacquered
white, red, or blue.
H 30", L 14", D 11" (76 x 35.5 x 28 cm)
Producer: Artek

2-397
Series 7, Child's Chair
Design: FH 2005 (based on Arne Jacobsen design, 1955)
Laminated plywood, many colors, stains or natural finish; available
with arms and swivel base.
H 24", L 15¾", D 16½" (60 x 40 x 42 cm)
Producer: Fritz Hansen

2-398

2-398
Boge
Design: Kristian Eriksson, 2004
Birch or oak cabinet, opens into table or desk.
H 27¾", L 30", D 27½"
(70.5 x 76.2 x 70 cm)
Producer: G.A.D.

2-399
#NE60 Child's Stool
Design: Alvar Aalto, 1932–33
Natural lacquered birch, birch veneer seat, linoleum, laminate, fabric or leather upholstered seat; companion design to adult tables and stools.
H 12½", 13¼", or 15" (32, 34, 38 cm)
Producer: Artek

2-399

2-400
Sleepi Convertible Crib
Design: Grønlund & Hvid
Natural beech, on wheels; converts to cot,
bed, or settee as child grows.
H 33", L 50", W 29" (85½ x 127½ x 74 cm)
Producer: Stokke

2-401
Tripp Trapp
Design: Peter Opsvik, 1972
Beech, ten colors and eight cushion fab-
rics; seat adjusts as child grows.
H 31½", L 18", D 19" (78½ x 45½ x 49 cm)
Producer: Stokke

2-400

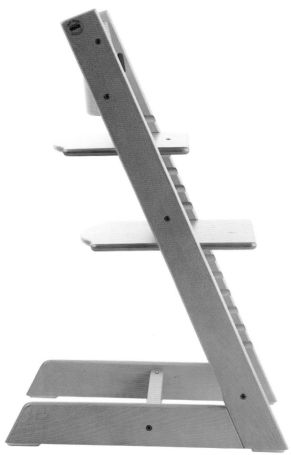

2-401

2-402

2-402
#8000 Series Child's Furniture
Design: Rud Thygesen & Johnny Sørensen, 1981
Laminated lacquered beech frame, fire-retardant upholstery,
linoleum, laminate, or beech-stave tabletop and seats; stackable.
Table: H 21", Diam. 23½" (53 x 60 cm)
Chair: H 21", Diam. 16½" (55 x 42 cm)
Stool: H 13", Diam 16¼" (33 x 41.5 cm)
Producer: Magnus Olesen

2-403
Keep Storage System
Design: Stokke
Flexible modules for children's rooms.
Laminated beech, natural, cherry, or
whitewash finish.
H 47", L 31½", D 11" (top), 23" (base)
(120 x 80 x 30–60 cm)
Producer: Stokke

2-404
Swing 6500
Design: Peter Opsvik
Wood and rope; four versions: suspended
or freestanding on own frame.
Producer: Håg

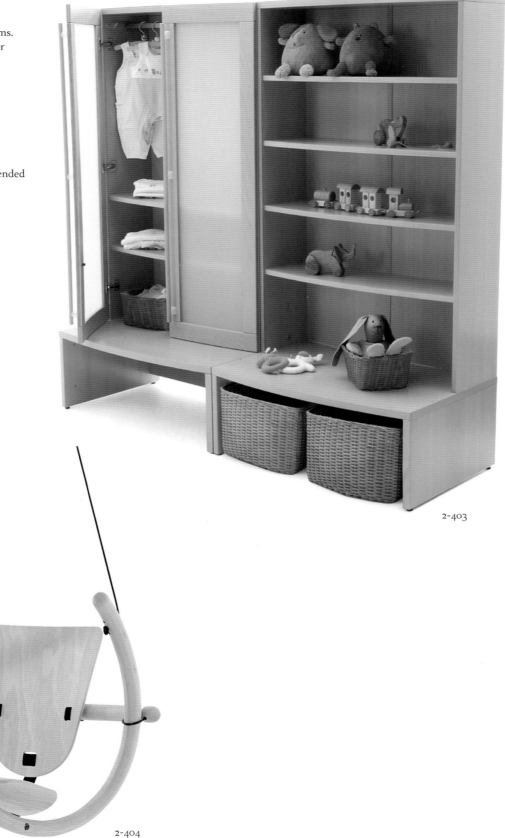

2-403

2-404

PART III

Appendices

Nordic Furniture Producers

Aero Design Furniture Oy
Yrjönkatu B, 00120 Helsinki, Finland
www.aerodesignfurniture.fi

Brødrene Andersen Møbelsnedkeri A/S
Lystrupvej 48, 8240 Risskov, Denmark
www.brdr-andersen.dk

Karl Andersson & Söner AB
Box 173, 561 22 Huskvarna, Sweden
www.karl-andersson.se

Artek
Eteläesplanadi 18, 00130 Helsinki, Finland
www.artek.fi

Avarte Oy
Hiekkakiventie 2, 00710 Helsinki, Finland
www.avarte.fi

Axelsen A/S
Byvejen 21, 5620 Glamsbjerg, Denmark
www.axelsen-dk.com

Erik Boisen A/S
Fabriksvej 15, 6650 Brørup, Denmark
www.erik-boisen.dk

Blå Station AB
Box 100, 296 22 Åhus, Sweden
www.blastation.se

Bo-Ex Møbler ApS
Frederikssundvej 157, 2700 Brønshoøj, Denmark
www.bo-ex.dk

The Canemaker (div. of JV Holding)
Moellegaardsparken 4, 8355 Solbjerg, Denmark
www.arnejacobsenfurniture.com

Jørgen Christensens Snedkeri A/S
Markstykkevej 16, 2610 Rødovre, Denmark
www.jcsnedkeri.dk

Cinal ApS (div. of Gubi)
Laplandsgade 4, 2300 Copenhagen S, Denmark
www.cinal.dk

David Design
Skeppsbron 3, 211-20 Malmö, Sweden
www.daviddesign.se

N. Eilersen A/S
Fabriksvej 2, 5485 Skamby, Denmark
www.eilersen-furniture.com

Engelbrechts
Skindergade 38, 1159 Copenhagen, Denmark
www.engelbrechts.com

EFG (European Furniture Group AB)
Trehörhavägen 2, P.O. Box 1017, 573 28 Tranås, Sweden
www.efg.se

Fjordfiesta Furniture
Fuglsetbakken 41, 6416 Molde, Norway
www.fjordfiesta.com

Flindt Design
Worsaaesvej 14, 1972 Fredriksberg C, 26709918, Denmark
www.flindtdesign.dk

Fora Form
P O Box 4. 6150 Ørsta, Norway
www.foraform.no

Formverk OY
Annankatu 5, 00120 Helsinki
www.formverk.com

Fredericia Furniture A/S
Treldevej 183, 7000 Fredericia, Denmark
www.fredericia.com

Front Design
Tegelviksgatan 20, 116 41 Stockholm, Sweden
www.frontdesign.se

G.A.D. AB
Södra Kyrkogatan 16, 621 56 Visby, Sweden
www.gad.se

Gärsnäs AB
Birger Jarlsgatan 57, 113 56, Stockholm, Sweden
www.garsnas.se

Getama Danmark A/S
Holmmarkvej 5, 9631 Gedsted, Denmark
www.getama.dk

Globe Furniture A/S
Marselis Boulevard 9, 8000 Aarhus C, Denmark
www.globefurniture.net

Gubi Int. ApS
Grønnegade 10, 1107 Copenhagen K, Denmark
www.gubi.dk

LK Hjelle Møbelfabrikk A/S
Postboks 8, 6239 Sykkylven, Norway
www.hjelle.no

Fritz Hansen A/S
Allerødvej 8, 3450 Allerød, Denmark
www.fritzhansen.com

Carl Hansen & Søn Møbelfabrik A/S
Holmevænget 8, 5560 Aarup, Denmark
www.carlhansen.com

Håg
Pb. 5055 Majorstuen, 0301 Oslo, Norway
www.hag.no

Hansen & Sørensen ApS
Vesterled 19, 6950 Ringkøbing, Denmark
www.hansensorensen.com

Iform
Sundspromenaden 27, Box 5055, 200 71 Malmö, Sweden
www.iform.net

Inno Interior OY
Tähdenlennontie 9, 02240 Espoo, Finland
www.inno.fi

C. N. Jorgensens Møbelsnedkeri
Hadsundvej 7, 2610 Rodøvre, Denmark

Erik Jørgensen Møbelfabrik A/S
Industrivænget 1, 5700 Svendborg, Denmark
www.erik-joergensen.com

Johanson Design AB
Hässleholmsvägen 28, 285 35 Markaryd, Sweden
www.johansondesign.se

Källemo AB
Box 605, 331 26 Värnamo, Sweden
www.kallemo.se

Kallin & Franzén
Börstiguägen 21, 520 26 Trädet, Sweden
www.kallinfranzen.se

Kinnarps
521 88 Kinnarp, Sweden
www.kinnarps.se

Kircodan Furniture A/S
Skodsborgvej 234, 2850 Nærum, Denmark
www.kircodan.com

Aksel Kjaersgaard
Strandvejen 158, 8300 Odder, Denmark
www.ak.dk

Klaessons Möbler AB
Box 18, 716 21 Fjugesta, Norway
www.klaessons.com

Hkt-Korhonen OY
Uusi - Littoistentie 2-4, 20660 Littoinen, Finland
www.hkt-korhonen.fi

Bent Krogh A/S
Grønlandsvej 5, Postboks 520, 8660 Skanderborg, Denmark
www.bent-krogh.dk

Lammhults Möbel AB
Box 26, 360 30 Lammhult, Sweden
www.lammhults.se

Lepo Product OY
Arkadiankatu 31, 00100 Helsinki, Finland
www.lepoproduct.fi

J. L. Møllers Møblefabrik A/S
Oddervej 202, 8270 Højberg, Denmark
www.jlm.dk

Martela Oy
Takkatie 1, PL 44, 00371 Helsinki, Finland
www.martela.fi

Mobel Original Design OY
PL 870, 20101 Turkku, Finland
www.mobel.net

Mokasser Furniture (formerly Leads)
P.O. Box 8, 6222 Ikonnes, Norway
www.mokasser.com

Montana Møbler A/S
Akkerupvej 16, 5683 Hårby, Denmark
www.montana.dk

Move Möbler AB
Glädjebacksgatan 7, 213 45 Trelleborg, Sweden
www.movemobler.com

Muurame
Pikitie 2, 15560 Nastola, Finland
www.muurame.com

Norrgavel
Lilla Södergatan 15, ög 223 53 Lund, Sweden
www.norrgavel.se

Offecct
Box 100, 543 21 Tibro, Sweden
www.offecct.se

Magnus Olesen A/S
Agertoft 2, Durup, 7870 Roslev, Denmark
www.magnus-olesen.dk

P.J. Furniture A/S
Højerupvej 30, 4660 Store-Heddinge, Denmark
www.pj-furniture.com

PP Møbler Aps
Toftevej 30, 3450 Allerød, Denmark
www.ppdk.com

Piiroinen
Tehdaskatu 28, 24100 Salo, Finland
www.piiroinen.com

Rud. Rasmussen
Noerrebrogade 45, 2200 Copenhagen N, Denmark
www.rudrasmussen.dk

Skandiform AB
Dolinvägen, 288 34 Vinslöv, Sweden
www.skandiform.se

Søborg Møbelfabrik A/S
Gladsaxevej 400, 2860 Søborg, Denmark
www.soeborg-moebler.dk

Softline A/S
Kidnakken 7, 4930 Maribo, Denmark
www.softline.dk

Sólóhusgögn Ehf
Armula 1, 108 Reykjavik, Iceland
www.solo.is

Stalidjan Ehf
Smidjuvegur 5, graen gata, 200 Kópavogur, Iceland

Stokke Gruppen AS
Hahjem, 6260 Skodje, Norway
www.stokke.com

Stouby A/S
Gl. Præstegårdsvej 8 F, 8723 Løsning, Denmark
www.stouby.com

Svenskt Tenn
Strangvägen 5, PO Box 5478, 114 84, Stockholm, Sweden
www.svenskttenn.se

Swedese
Box 156, 567 23 Vaggeryd, Sweden
www.swedese.se

Tranekær Furniture A/S
Ndr. Løkkebyvej 1, Tullebølle, 5953 Tranekær, Denmark
www.tranekaer-furniture.com

Trioline AS-Bahnsen Collection
Holmevej 10, 5a683 Hårby, Denmark
www.trioline.com

Variér Furnitureas
Håhjem, 6260 Skodje, Norway
www.varierfurniture.com

Vivero OY
Hämeentie 11, 00530 Helsinki, Finland
www.vivero.fi

Designer Biographies

Note: This listing includes furniture designers past and present, and is as comprehensive as possible within the limitations of space and available information. Career details are selective, and were drawn primarily from current sources, including manufacturer catalogs, website interviews and published references.

AAGARD ANDERSEN, GUNNAR, Danish, 1919–1982
Training: Skolen for Kunsthåndvaerk, Copenhagen, 1936–39; Konstakademiet, Stockholm, 1939; Det Kongelige Danske Kunstakademi, Copenhagen, 1940–46
Designs Produced By: Fredericia, Fritz Hansen, Rud. Rasmussen
Exhibitions, Honors, Other Distinctions: Bindesbøll prize; Danmarks Nationalbank Jubilee prize. Works in many museum collections.

AALTO, ALVAR, Finnish, 1898–1976
Training: Technillinen Korkeakoulu, Helsinki, 1916–21
Designs Produced By: Artek, Iittala
Exhibitions, Honors, Other Distinctions: 1923 Established design office; 1935 Founded Artek (with Harry and Marie Gullichsen); 1935 Royal Institute of British Architects, gold medal; 1939 designed Finnish Pavilion, New York Worlds Fair; 1938 Exhibition at Museum of Modern Art, New York; 1937 designed Finnish Pavilion, Exposition Internationale des Arts Décoratifs, Paris; 1933 Exhibition, Fortnum and Mason, London. Professor of architecture at Massachusetts Institute of Technology 1946–48. Elected to Finnish Academy, 1955; named president of Finnish Academy, 1963–68. First Nordic architect to be internationally recognized, represented in museum collections worldwide, with glassware as well as furniture designs.

ACKING, CARL-AXEL, Swedish, 1910–2001
Training: Konstfackskolan, Stockholm, 1930–34
Designs Produced By: NK, Bodafors
Exhibitions, Honors, Other Distinctions: 1952 Lunning Prize; 1939 exhibited at New York World's Fair; 1937 Exposition Internationale des Arts Décoratifs et Techniques dans la Vie Moderne, Paris; 1936 Triennale di Milano.

ALLARD, GUNILLA, Swedish, born 1957
Training: Konstfackskolan, Stockholm 1983–88; Det Kongelige Danske Kunstakademi, Copenhagen 1985
Designs Produced By: Lammhults, Marbodal, Kasthall Mattor & Golv, Orrefors, Zero
Exhibitions, Honors, Other Distinctions: 2001 Swedish Interior Architects award; 2000, 1999, 1995, 1992 Excellent Swedish Form; 2000 Blueprint 100% Design, London; 1996 Bruno Mathsson Prize, 1996 Georg Jensen Prize. Exhibitions in Denmark, Sweden, London, Tokyo; work in collections including Nationalmuseum, Stockholm, and Röhsska Museet, Göteborg.

ALMÉN, TONY, Swedish, born 1963
Designs Produced By: Karl Andersson

ANDERSSEN, TORBJØRN, Norwegian, born 1976
Training: Kunsthøyskolen, Bergen, 1997–2002
Designs Produced By: LK Hjelle, Globe, Iform, Offect, Swedese
Exhibitions, Honors, Other Distinctions: 2000–5 Norwegian Design Council; 2004 *Wallpaper* Interior Design award; 2003 Bruno Mathsson award, *Elle* Designer of the Year; international exhibitions in Tokyo, Stockholm, London, Brussels, New York, and Milan; 2003 established Norway Says (with Andreas Engesrik and Espen Voll)

ANTTONEN, SARI, Finnish, born 1966
Training: Vihti Art and Craft College, 1986–88; Taideteollinen Korkeakoulu Helsinki, 1990
Designs Produced By: Piiroinen
Exhibitions, Honors, Other Distinctions: 1996 Finnish National Prize for Young Architects; 1994 IKEA Competition (1st). 1997 Founded Reflex Design Ltd. (Helsinki and Paris).

ARBÉN, LOVE, Swedish, born 1962
Training: Kungliga Tekniska Högskolan, 1978; Konstfack, both
    Stockholm
Designs Produced By: Lammhults
Exhibitions, Honors, Other Distinctions: 1991 Forsnäs Prize,
    Sweden; 1991, 1989, 1988, and 1983 Excellent Swedish Form.
    Works in Nationalmuseum, Stockholm, and Röhsska
    Museet, Göteborg.

ARNIO, EERO, Finnish, born 1932
Training: Taideteollinen Korkeakoulu, Helsinki,
    1954–57
Designs Produced By: Asko, Adelta
Exhibitions, Honors, Other Distinctions: 1991 Masters of
    Modern Design, New York; 1968 American Institute of
    Interior Designers award. Represented in permanent collec-
    tions in major museums worldwide.

ASIKAINEN, KARI, Finnish, born 1939
Training: University of Helsinki, 1966
Designs Produced By: P. O. Korhonen
Exhibitions, Honors, Other Distinctions: 1984 Finnish
    Government Design Prize; 1982 SIO Design Prize.

ASIKAINEN, TEPPO, Finnish, born 1968
Designs Produced By: Offecct
Exhibitions, Honors, Other Distinctions: 2000 Young Nordic
    Design: The Generation X international traveling exhibi-
    tion.

ASPLUND, ERIK GUNNAR, Swedish 1885–1940
Training: Kungliga Tekniska Högskolan, Stockholm,
    1905–9
Designs Produced By: Källemo
Exhibitions, Honors, Other Distinctions: 1917 Home exhi-
    bition, Stockholm; 1925 Exposition Internationale des
    Arts Décoratifs et Industriels Modernes, Paris; 1930 Chief
    Architect, Stockholm Fair; 1988 Exhibition Gunnar
    Asplund, A Great Modern Architect, London. Work in
    major museums and international exhibitions. Known pri-
    marily as architect, introduced the concept of functionalist
    modernism to Sweden. Also a professor and editor.

AXELSSON, ÅKE, Swedish, born 1932
Training: Visby Verkstadsskola, 1947–51; Konstfack,
    Stockholm, 1952–57
Designs Produced By: Gärsnäs
Exhibitions, Honors, Other Distinctions: 1997–95 Chair exhi-
    bition, Paris, Copenhagen, various Swedish venues; 1995
    Bruno Mathsson Prize; 1994 Prince Eugene Medal; 1993,
    1992, 1988, 1985 Excellent Swedish Form; 1993 Gärsnäs
    Jubilee Competition; 1978 Nordic Design Competition,
    Copenhagen; 1988 Faces of Swedish Design touring exhibi-
    tion, United States; many other exhibitions. Member of
    Royal Academy of Fine Arts, Stockholm. 1962 Established
    own design practice.

BERLIN, BORIS, Danish, born 1953 (Leningrad)
Training: Leningrad Institute of Applied Arts and Design
Designs Produced By: Bent Krogh, Fora Form, Klaessons,
    Swedese
Exhibitions, Honors, Other Distinctions: 2004 Red Dot
    Design Award, Germany; Forsnäs Prize, Sweden; 2000 Bo
    Bedre furniture prize, 100% Design/Blueprint Award, Best
    of NeoCon, Furniture design Prize; 1996 Forsnäs Prize
    Sweden (2nd); 1993 Danish National Art Foundation; 1992
    Norwegian Design Council; 1991 TOP Danmark, G-Mark,
    Japan, Scandinavian Furniture design Award. Also designs
    glass, industrial objects. 1983 Established Komplot Design
    (in partnership with Poul Christensen).

BERNSTRAND, THOMAS, Swedish, born 1965
Training: Inchbald School of Design, London,
    1988–89; Danmarks Designskole, Copenhagen,
    1996; Konstfack, Stockholm, 1994–99; Konsthögskolan,
    Stockholm 2005–06
Designs Produced By: Swedese
Exhibitions, Honors, Other Distinctions: 2005 Designer of
    the Year Elle Decor Sweden, Svenskt Tenn award; 2005
    exhibitions at Nationalmuseum, Stockholm; H55 pavilion,
    Helsingborg, Sweden; 1998, 2000, 2002 Excellent Swedish
    Form; 1998 Young Swedish Design Award; 2004 Design in
    Sweden exhibition, London, England; 2002 Röhsska Museet,
    Göteborg; 2000 Young Nordic Design: The Generation X
    international traveling exhibition, others. Designs exhibi-
    tions, interiors, glass, lighting.

BERNT [PETERSEN], Danish, born 1937
Training: In cabinetmaking 1957; Kunsthändvaerkerskolen,
    1960; Skolen for Brugkunst, 1973 (both Copenhagen)
Designs Produced By: Getama, Søborg, C. J. Christensen
Exhibitions, Honors, Other Distinctions: 1998 Good Design
    Award, Japan; 1988 Danish Forestry Competition (2nd);
    1987, 1976, 1972 Danish State Art Foundation; 1977 furni-
    ture prize, Denmark; 1972 Foght Foundation; 1970 Danish
    Arts and Crafts Annual Award; 1969 Danish Furniture
    Manufacturer's Association; 1966 Illum Foundation.

BEUCHEL, MONI, Swedish, born 1964
Training: Nyckelviksskolan, Lidingö; Konstfack, Stockholm,
    1998–2003
Designs Produced By: Karl Andersson

BOHLIN, JONAS, Swedish, born 1953
Training: Aso Technical College, 1970–74; Konstfack,
    Stockholm, 1981
Designs Produced By: Kållemo
Exhibitions, Honors, Other Distinctions: 2001 Excellent
    Swedish Form; 1997 Design Nordic Way traveling exhibition,
    Sweden; 1997, 1994 grants from Swedish State Fund for Arts;
    1988 Georg Jensen Prize; Excellent Swedish Form traveling
    exhibition, United States; 1985 New Swedish Furniture,
    New York; 1981 Swedish Society of Crafts and Design. Works
    in collections including Centre Culturel Suedois, Paris;
    Kunstindustrimuseet, Copenhagen; Malmö Kontsmuseer;
    Musikaliska Akademien; Nationalmuseum, Stockholm;
    Röhsska Museet, Göteborg; and other group exhibitions.
    1983 Established own office. Also designs lighting.

BORGERSEN, TORE, Norwegian, born 1966
Designs Produced By: David Design, Globe, Hovden, Iform, LK Hjelle, Swedese, Vestre
Exhibitions, Honors, Other Distinctions: 2004 International Design Award; 2003 Group exhibition, Totem Design, New York; 2002 Stockholm International Fair; 2001 Salone Internazionale del Mobile, Milan; 2001, 2000 Designers Block, London. Member, Norway Says.

BØRRE, PER, Danish, born 1948
Training: Kunsthåandvaerkerskolen, 1974; Det Kongelige Danske Kunstakademi, Copenhagen, 1981
Designs Produced By: Fredericia
Exhibitions, Honors, Other Distinctions: Instructor, Danmarks Designskole; 1984 IBD Gold Award, New York. 1982 Established own design studio.

BORSELIUS, STEFAN, Swedish, born 1974
Training: Cabinetmaking schools 1990–93; Stenebyskolan, 1993–98 in cabinetry, then furniture restoration; Carl Malmsten Skola, 1998–2000; Konstfack, Stockholm, MFA, 2000–02
Designs Produced By: Blå Station
Exhibitions, Honors, Other Distinctions: 2005 Salone Internazionale del Mobile, Milan, Swedish Style, Tokyo, Design in Sweden, London; 2004 Red Dot award, Germany; 2004 Design in Sweden, Museum of London, *Sköna Hem* Product of the Year; 2003 Swedish EDIDA award, Goldenchair, Swedish architect award; 2000 Young Swedish design award. Work in collection of Nationalmuseum, Stockholm.

BRATTRUD, HANS, Norwegian, born 1933
Training: School of Arts, Crafts and Design, Oslo, 1952–57
Designs Produced By: Fjord Fiesta

BUSK, FLEMMING, Danish, born 1967
Training: School of Architecture, Århus, Denmark, 2000
Designs Produced By: David, Globe, Softline
Exhibitions, Honors, Other Distinctions: Designs represented at the Royal House of Norway, the Norwegian Embassy in Helsinki, and the Carnegie Trust. 2000 Established Busk+Hertzog (with Stephan B. Hertzog).

CAMPBELL, LOUISE, Danish, born 1970
Training: Kunsthändvaerkerskolen, Copenhagen; London College of Furniture Design
Designs Produced By: Bahnsen Collection, Erik Jørgensens, Holmegaard, Louis Poulsen
Exhibitions, Honors, Other Distinctions: 2005 *Bo Bedre* Designer of Year; 2004 Finn Juhl Prize, IF-Prize, Hanover, Nordic Cool, Hot Women Designers, Washington, D.C.; 2003 Scandinavian Design Beyond the Myth traveling exhibition, Europe; 2003 State Arts Council Award, Red Dot Design Award, Germany; *Bo Bedre* Element 99; 2000 Young Nordic Design: The Generation X international traveling exhibition. Also designs lighting.

CELSING, JOHAN, Swedish, born 1955
Training: Architecture Kungliga Tekniska Högskolan, Stockholm, 1975–80; Académie de la Grande Chaumière, Paris, 1977–78; ILAUD, Urbino, 1980
Designs Produced By: Gärsnäs
Exhibitions, Honors, Other Distinctions: 2002, 1997, 1995, 1994 Excellent Swedish Form; 1998 Architektur im 20. Jahrhundert, Frankfurt am Main, Stockholm, Architecture Biennial, Buenos Aires; 1997 New Generation of the North, Helsinki, Oslo, Copenhagen, Venice, and other cities; 1995 Tengbom Prize, Swedish Royal Academy of Arts.

CHRISTIANSEN, POUL, Danish, born 1947
Training: Det Kongelige Danske Kunstakademi, Arkitektskolen, 1973
Designs Produced By: Bent Krogh, Fora Form, Formverk, Klaessons, Le Klint, Swedese
Exhibitions, Honors, Other Distinctions: 2004 Red Dot Design Award, Germany; 2004 Forsnäs Prize, Sweden; 2003 100% Design / Blueprint Award; *Bo Bedre* furniture prize, Denmark; 2003 Best of NeoCon, Chicago; 2002 Furniture design Prize, Denmark; 1992 Mark of Good Design, Norway; 1991 TOP Danmark, G-Mark, Japan, Scandinavian Furniture Award. Also lighting, industrial design. 1983 Established, Komplot Design (with Boris Berlin).

CHRISTIANSSON, ULLA, Swedish, born 1938
Training: Konstfackskolan, Stockholm
Designs Produced By: Karl Andersson
Exhibitions, Honors, Other Distinctions: Represented in various exhibitions including Excellent Swedish Design.

CLAESSON, MÅRTEN, Swedish, born 1970
Training: Konstfack, Stockholm 1994; Parsons School of Design, New York, 1992; Vasa Technical College, Stockholm, 1988
Designs Produced By: David Design, Formverk, Offecct, Swedese
Exhibitions, Honors, Other Distinctions: 1995 Forsnäs Prize; multiple honors (as CKR) for furniture design, exhibitions, interior design. 1993 Established Claesson Koivisto Rune (with Eero Koivisto and Ola Rune).

DAHLSTRÖM, BJÖRN, Swedish, born 1957
Designs Produced By: Källemo, Cbi, Ericsson, Hackman, Playsam, Scania, Skeppshult
Exhibitions, Honors, Other Distinctions: 1991–98 Excellent Swedish Form; 1993–98 Group exhibitions (Berlin, Stockholm, New York, London, Frankfurt); 1996 Plus Design, Germany; 1995 *Sköna Hem* furniture design of the year. Works in various collections including Röhsska Museet, Göteborg, and Victoria and Albert Museum, London.

DITZEL, JØRGEN, Danish, 1921–1961
Training: Kunsthändvaerkerskolen, 1944; Det Kongelige Danske Kunstakademi (both Copenhagen)
Designs Produced By: Pierantonio Bonacina, Herning weaving mills, Georg Jensen, Kold sawmills, Ravenholm, Unika Vaev
Exhibitions, Honors, Other Distinctions: 1960 Triennale di

Milano (gold medal), 1957, 1954, 1951 (silver medals), all with Nanna Ditzel; 1956 Lunning Prize, with Nanna Ditzel.

DITZEL, NANNA, Danish, 1923–2005
Training: Trained as cabinetmaker, 1943; Det Kongelige Danske Kunstakademi, 1945; Kunsthändvaerkerskolen, 1946 (both Copenhagen)
Designs Produced By: Fredericia, Getama, Georg Jensen, Knud Willadsen, Pierantonio Bonacina, Ravnholm, Softline.
Exhibitions, Honors, Other Distinctions: 1999 Thorvald Bindesbøll Prize; 1995 ID Prize; 1990 International Furniture Design Competition (silver medal); 1960 Triennale di Milano (gold medal), 1957, 1954, 1951 (silver medals), all with Jorgen Ditzel; 1956 Lunning Prize, with Jørgen Ditzel; 1950 Cabinetmakers' Guild (1st), Goldsmith's Association. Also designed silver hollowware, jewelry, textiles.

DRANGER, JAN, Swedish, born 1941
Training: Konstfack, Stockholm, 1968
Designs Produced By: Dranger Design, IKEA, Innovator
Exhibitions, Honors, Other Distinctions: 1999 Good Swedish Design.

DYSTHE, SVEN IVAR, Norwegian, born 1931
Training: Royal College of Art, London
Designs Produced By: Fora Form
Exhibitions, Honors, Other Distinctions: 1989 Jacobs Prize, Norway; other recognitions.

EILERSEN, JENS JUUL, Danish, born 1938
Designs Produced By: Eilersen
Exhibitions, Honors, Other Distinctions: Numerous awards for innovative upholstered furniture designs, many of which have been patented.

EKLUND, HENNING, Swedish, born 1968
Training: School of Design and Crafts at Göteborg University, 1998
Designs Produced By: Klaessons
Designs in partnership with Kajsa Nordstrom.

EKSTRAND, RUUD, Swedish, born 1943
Designs Produced By: David
Exhibitions, Honors, Other Distinctions: 1992 Guldstolen; 1986 Forsnäs Prize, Sweden, Excellent Swedish Form. Works have been exhibited in Sweden and Tokyo museums.

EKSTRÖM, TERJE, Norwegian, born 1944
Training: Statens Håndverks-og Kunstindustriskole, Oslo, 1968
Designs Produced By: Stokke
Exhibitions, Honors, Other Distinctions: Represented in major exhibitions and design collections. 1977 Established own studio.

EKSTRÖM, YNGVE, Swedish, 1913–1988
Designs Produced By: Swedese
Exhibitions, Honors, Other Distinctions: 1945 Founded Swedese Möbler. 1999 Lamino chair named best twentieth-century Swedish Furniture design. Excellent Swedish Form (numerous awards); other international honors. Work shown in special exhibitions in many museums; designs in collections including Victoria and Albert Museum and Nationalmuseum, Stockholm.

ELDOY, OLAV, Norwegian, born 1948
Training: Kunsthåndtverkskole, Bergen, 1973
Designs Produced By: Fora Form, Møre
Exhibitions, Honors, Other Distinctions: 2003 Salon Deux Meuble Paris; 2000-2, 1986, 1977 Mark of Good Design, Norway; 1997 Design Nordic Way exhibition, Sweden.

ENGESVIK, ANDREAS, Norwegian, born 1970
Training: Kunsthøyskolen, Bergen, 1995–2000; Statsuniversitet, Bergen, 1991–1995
Designs Produced By: LK Hjelle, Iform, Offecct, Swedese, Globe
Exhibitions, Honors, Other Distinctions: 2000–5 honored by Norwegian Design Council; 2004 *Wallpaper* Interior design award; Bruno Mathsson award; 2003 *Elle* Designer of the Year; 2001, 2000 Salone Internazionale del Mobile, Milan; Designers Block, London. Work exhibited in Tokyo, Stockholm, Brussels, and New York. 2003 Established Norway Says (with Torbjørn Anderssen and Espen Voll).

ERIKSSON, THOMAS, Swedish, born 1959
Training: Konstfack, Stockholm
Designs Produced By: Offecct
Exhibitions, Honors, Other Distinctions: 1988 Founder, TEArk; 1988 Co-founder, Stockholm Design Lab.

ERNST, MORTEN, Danish, born 1964
Training: Det Kongelige Danske Kunstakademi, Copenhagen
Designs Produced By: Erik Jørgensen
Exhibitions, Honors, Other Distinctions: 2001 Red Dot Award, Germany. Practices in partnership with Anne-Mette Jensen.

FABRICIUS, PREBEN, Danish, 1931–1984
Training: Trained as cabinetmaker with Niels Vodder, Copenhagen; Skolen for Boligindretning, Copenhagen, 1959
Designs Produced By: Bo-ex, Ivan Schlechter
Exhibitions, Honors, Other Distinctions: 1969 Illum Prize. 1962–70 Partnership with Jørgen Kastholm.

FLINDT, CHRISTIAN, Danish
Designs Produced By: Flindt Design
Exhibitions, Honors, Other Distinctions: 2005 *Bo Bedre* design award, Copenhagen Furniture Fair Prize, Danish National Bank Jubilee Grant (also 2004, 2002); 2003 IDEE Design Competition for Tokyo Designers Block.

FOERSOM, JØHANNES, Danish, born 1947
Training: In cabinetmaking, 1964–69; Kunsthåandvaerkerskolen, Copenhagen, 1972
Designs Produced By: Erik Boisen, Erik Jørgensen, Fredericia, Hansen & Sørensen
Exhibitions, Honors, Other Distinctions: 2005 Finn Juhl Prize (with Peter Hiort-Lorenzen); 2002, 2000 Excellent Swedish Form; 1999, 1995, 1994, 1992 Red Dot Awards, Germany; 1998

Bruno Mathsson Award; 1995 Best of NeoCon, Chicago; 1994 Forsnäs Prize, Sweden. From 1971, partnership with Peter Hiort-Lorenzen.

FÖRSTER, MONICA, Swedish, born 1966
Training: Beckmans School of Design, 1995; Konstfack, 1997 (both Stockholm)
Designs Produced By: David Design, Offecct, Skruf
Exhibitions, Honors, Other Distinctions: 1999, 1998 Sweden Innovation Centre Grant. Work in exhibitions in Stockholm, Milan, Munich, Sydney, London.

FRANK, JOSEF, Austrian, 1885–1967 (born Vienna)
Training: Technical Institute, Vienna, 1910
Designs Produced By: Svenskt Tenn
Exhibitions, Honors, Other Distinctions: 1952, 20 Years at Svenskt Tenn, National Museum, Stockholm; 1965 Austrian national architecture prize Vienna; 1939 exhibited at New York World's Fair; 1937 exhibited at Exposition Internationale des Arts Décoratifs et Techniques dans la Vie Moderne, Paris; 1999 Josef Frank, Architect, exhibition, New York. 1919–25 professor, Wiener Kunstgewerbeschule, Vienna; 1941–46 professor, New School for Social Research, New York. Also celebrated as an architect and textile designer.

FÜRST, CHRISTINA, Swedish, born 1950
Training: Konstfackskolen, Nyckelviksskolan, both Stockholm
Designs Produced By: Karl Andersson

GAMMELGAARD, JØRGEN, Danish, 1938–1991
Training: Apprentice cabinetmaker, 1957; Kunsthåndvaerkerskolen, 1959–62; Kinstakademiets Arkitektskole, 1962–64 (all Copenhagen)
Designs Produced By: Erik Jørgensen, Karl Andersson, Rodolfo, Børg Schiang
Exhibitions, Honors, Other Distinctions: 1986 Danish Design Center award; 1971 Furniture Prize, Denmark. Worked for Grete Jalk, Steen Eiler Rasmussen, Mogens Koch and Arne Jacobsen. 1973 Established own design office.

GAMMELGAARD, NIELS, Danish, born 1944
Training: Det Kongelige Danske Kunstakademiet, 1970
Designs Produced By: Bent Krogh, Erik Jørgensen, Fora Form, Fritz Hansen, P. O. Korhonen, Softline
Exhibitions, Honors, Other Distinctions: 1998 Danish Design Center award Årspris; 1996 Red Dot Award, Germany; 1996, 1991, 1990 I.D. Prize; 1993 Danish Furniture Prize; 1991 G-Mark, Japan; 1986, 1984 Excellent Swedish Form, many others. 1978–86 and from 1992, practice as Pelikan Design (with Lars Mathiesen).

GEHL, EBBE, Danish, born 1942
Training: Rud. Rasmussen cabinetmaking workshop, 1959–63; Kunsthandverkskolen, Copenhagen, 1963–66
Designs Produced By: Carl Hansen, A. Mikael Laursen, Aksel Kjersgaard, P. J. Furniture
Exhibitions, Honors, Other Distinctions: Numerous medals, awards, grants and honors. Exhibitions in Denmark, Europe, Japan, and United States. 1970 Established partnership (with Søren Nissen).

GEST, PETER, Swedish, born 1963
Designs Produced By: Karl Anderson
Practices in partnership with Tony Almén.

GNEIB, ANKI, Swedish, born 1965
Training: Konstfack, Stockholm
Designs Produced By: Offecct
Exhibitions, Honors, Other Distinctions: 2005 Swedish Style Milan, Italy; 2004 Nordic Cool, Hot Women Designers, Washington, D.C., Swedish New Glass, New York; 2003 Transformations, New York; 1996 Excellent Swedish Form, Stockholm.

GUðMUNDSDÓTTIR, DÖGG, Icelandic, born 1970
Designs Produced By: Dögg Design, Solohusgogn
Exhibitions, Honors, Other Distinctions: Work featured in exhibitions of new Nordic design.

GUSTAFSSON, SIGURDUR, Icelandic, born 1962
Training: Oslo School of Architecture, 1990
Designs Produced By: Källemo AB
Exhibitions, Honors, Other Distinctions: 2001 Bruno Mathsson Prize; 1999 Nordic Transparency, Stedeljik Museum, Amsterdam; 1996 DV design prize. Works in various collections including National Museum, Stockholm; Röhsska Museet, Göteborg; Malmö Art Museum; Stedeljik Museum, Amsterdam; National Museum of Armenia; Islands Designmuseum, Reykjavik. 1971 Established own architectural practice.

HAKALA, PENTTI, Finnish, born 1949
Training: Taideteollinen Korkekoulu Helsinki, 1982
Designs Produced By: HKT Korhonen, Avarte, Inno, Martelum, P. O. Korhonen
Exhibitions, Honors, Other Distinctions: 1995 group exhibition, Saarijärvi Art Museum; 1985, 1983 Finnish Furniture Prize, Finland.

HAKSTEEN, MARTIN, Norwegian
Designs Produced By: LK Hjelle
Exhibitions, Honors, Other Distinctions: 1999 Mark of Good Design, Norway.

HANSEN, ANDREAS, Danish, born 1936
Training: In cabinetmaking at Ringe, 1956; Kunsthåandvaerkerskolen, 1962; Det Kongelige Danske Kunstakademi, 1962–63, both Copenhagen
Designs Produced By: Brødrene Andersen, J. L. Møllers Møbelfabrik; Le Klint

HAUGESEN, NIELS JØRGEN, Danish, born 1936
Training: Cabinetmaking apprentice, 1956; Kunsthåandvaerkerskolen, Copenhagen, 1961, 1971

Designs Produced By: Bent Krogh, Fredericia,Fritz Hansen, Tranekær

Exhibitions, Honors, Other Distinctions: 1996 Furniture Prize, Denmark, 1989 Danish Industry Design Award; 1987, 1986 ID award; 1960, 1961, 1964, Cabinetmakers' Guild Exhibitions, Copenhagen. Work in collections including Det Danske Kunstindustrimuseet, Copenhagen, Stedelijk Museum, Amsterdam, Arts Décoratif Union Louvre, Paris, Die Neue Sammlung, Munich; and Kunstmuseet Trapholt.

HEIKKILA, SIMO, Finnish, born 1943
Training: Taideteollinen Oppilaitos, Helsinki, 1967
Designs Produced By: Inno, Klaessons, Asko
Exhibitions, Honors, Other Distinctions: 1999 Bruno Mathsson Prize; 1992 Forsnäs Prize, Sweden; 1989 SIO Furniture Award, Sweden; 1986 State Designer Prize; 1984 SIO Award, Copenhagen; 1981 Habitare Prize, Helsinki. Works in museum collections including Museum of Applied Arts, Helsinki; Kunstindustrimuseet, Oslo; Kunstindustrimuseet, Copenhagen; Röhsska Museet, Göteborg; Museum für Kunst und Gewerbe, Hamburg; Cooper-Hewitt Museum, New York; Victoria and Albert Museum, London.

HEIN, PIET, Danish, 1905–1996
Training: Kobenhavns Universitets, theoretical physics; Kungliga Teckniska Hogskolan, Stockholm
Designs Produced By: Fritz Hansen
Exhibitions, Honors, Other Distinctions: 1989 Danish Design Center award; 1972 Honorary Doctorate, Yale University; 1971 I.D. Prize; 1975 Alexander Graham Bell Silver Bell; 1968 I.D. Prize. Celebrated idiosyncratic poet, scientist and inventor as well as product designer.

HENNINGSEN, POUL, Danish, 1894–1967
Training: Danmarks Tekniske Højskole, 1911–14; Polyteckknick, 1914–17 (both Copenhagen)
Designs Produced By: Louis Poulsen
Exhibitions, Honors, Other Distinctions: 1925 Gold medal, Exposition Internationale des Art Décoratifs et Industriels Modernes, Paris. Lighting designs in exhibitions and museums worldwide. Also a poet, playwright, journalist, and founder of the critical journal *Kritisk Revy*.

HERMANSEN, ANDERS, Danish
Training: Danmarks Designskole, 1982
Designs Produced By: Bang & Olufsen, Paustian
Exhibitions, Honors, Other Distinctions: 1997, 1996 IF-Prize, Hanover; 1988 furniture prize, Denmark; 1984 State Art Fund award.

HERTZOG, STEPHAN BORGEN, Danish, born 1969
Designs Produced By: David, Globe

HIORT-LORENZEN, PETER, Danish, born 1943
Training: Kunsthåandvaerkerskolen, 1962–65; Det Kongelige Danske Kunstakadem, both Copenhagen
Designs Produced By: Erik Boisen, Erik Jørgensen, Fredericia, Lammhults, Skive

Exhibitions, Honors, Other Distinctions: 2005 Finn Juhl prize (with Jøhannes Foersom); 1998 Bruno Mathsson Award; 1995 Best Chair, NeoCon, Chicago; 1985 Furniture Prize, Denmark. 1971 Established partnership (with Jøhannes Foersom).

HJORT, AXEL EINAR, Swedish, 1888–1959
Designs Produced By: Nordiska Kompaniet
Exhibitions, Honors, Other Distinctions: From 1927 head of furniture design at NK, Stockholm; 1930 exhibited at Stockholm Fair.

HØJ, JØRGEN, Danish, 1925–1994
Training: As metalworker and upholsterer; Kunsthåandvaerkerskolen, 1950
Designs Produced By: Ivan Schlechter, Thorvald Madsen, PP Møbler

HOLMBERG, KAARLE, Finnish, born 1951
Designs Produced By: Lepo, Piiroinen

HÖVELSKOV, JÖRGEN, Danish, 1935–2005
Training: Cabinetmaking with Borge Mogensen, 1934; Kungliga Tekniska Högskolan, 1938–41
Designs Produced By: J. Christensens
Exhibitions, Honors, Other Distinctions: 1972 C. F. Handens medal, Denmark; 1963 Cabinetmakers Guild Exhibitions (1958 annual prize). Worked for Mogens Koch, Kaare Klint. 1950 Established own office.

HULDT, JOHAN, Swedish, born 1942
Training: Konstfack, Stockholm, 1964–68
Designs Produced By: Fogia, Innovator
Exhibitions, Honors, Other Distinctions: Former chairman, Svensk Form. 1972, 1973, 1974 Scandinavian Chair of the Year; 1974 Good Form, Germany. Work represented in many exhibitions. Designs in collection of Nationalmuseum, Stockholm; Museum of Modern Art, New York. 1968 Founded Innovator Design (with Jan Dranger); 1978 Founded Basic Design AB.

HVASS, NIELS, Swedish, born 1958
Training: Danmarks Designskole, furniture and tools, 1987
Practices as Strand+Hvass (with Christina Strand).

HVIDT, CHRISTIAN, Danish, born 1946
Training: Danmarks Tekniske Højskole, Copenhagen
Designs Produced By: Søborg, Fritz Hansen
Exhibitions, Honors, Other Distinctions: 2004 Cabinetmakers Prize.

HVIDT, FLEMMING, Danish, born 1944
Training: Kunsthåandvaerkerskolen, Copenhagen, 1970
Designs Produced By: Søborg, Flemming Hvidt
Exhibitions, Honors, Other Distinctions: 1979 Furniture Prize, Denmark; other awards for furniture and industrial design. Designs in museum collections including Museum of Modern Art, New York, Danish Arts Foundation and Trapholt Museum, Copenhagen.

HVIDT, PETER, Danish, 1916–1986
Training: Kunsthåndvaerkerskolen, Copenhagen, 1940
Designs Produced By: Fritz Hansen, Søborg, France & Son
Exhibitions, Honors, Other Distinctions: 1980 Scandinavian
    Modern Design, 1880–1980 traveling exhibition, United
    States and Canada; 1983 Design Since 1945, Philadelphia;
    1958 Formes Scandinaves, Paris; 1954, 1951 Triennale di
    Milano awards; 1951 Good Design, New York. Designed with
    Orla Mørgard-Nielsen, 1947–75.

JACOBSEN, ARNE, Danish, 1902–1971
Training: Tekniske Selskabs Skoler, 1924; Kongelige Danske
    Kunstakademi, Copenhagen, 1927
Designs Produced By: Fritz Hansen, Louis Poulsen, Stelton, A.
    Mikkelsen, and others
Exhibitions, Honors, Other Distinctions: 1925 Exposition
    Internationale des Art Décoratifs et Industriels Modernes,
    Paris; 1954–57 Design in Scandinavia traveling exhibition,
    United States and Canada; 1968 Formes Scandinaves, Paris;
    1960–61 Arts of Denmark, traveling exhibition, United
    States; 1957 Triennale di Milano grand prize; 1967 ID prize.
    Denmark; 1968 International Design Award, American
    Institute of Interior Designers, United States; 2002 retro-
    spective exhibitions marking one-hundredth celebration
    of his birth. Represented in major exhibitions and museum
    collections worldwide. One of Denmark's most celebrated
    modern architects, Jacobsen also designed tableware and
    other objects.

JAKOBSEN, HANS SANDGREN, Danish, born 1963
Training: Cabinetmaker apprentice to Viby J., 1986
Designs Produced By: Axelsen, Bent Krogh, Fritz Hansen,
    Fredericia
Exhibitions, Honors, Other Distinctions: 2000 G-Mark, Japan;
    2000 Young Nordic Design: The Generation X interna-
    tional traveling exhibition; 1999 Living Danish Design,
    London; 1999 Fosnäs Prize, Sweden, *Bo Bedre* furniture
    prize; 1998 Red Dot Award, Germany; 1995 Center for
    Dansk Kunsthåndværk (2nd). Worked as cabinetmaker
    at Rud. Rasmussens, Copenhagen, 1986, 1987; Danmarks
    Designskole, Copenhagen, 1986–90. Worked for Nanna
    Ditzel. 1997 Established own office.

JALK, GRETA, Danish, born 1920
Training: Kunsthåndvaerkerskolan, 1940–42; Det Kongelige
    Danske Kunstakademi, 1946 (under Kaare Klint) (both
    Copenhagen)
Designs Produced By: France & Søn, Fritz Hansen, Poul
    Jeppesen, Niels Roth Andersen
Exhibitions, Honors, Other Distinctions: 1946 First prize,
    Cabinetmakers' Guild competition. Designs in many exhibi-
    tions and museum collections worldwide.

JÄRVI, TEEMU, Finnish, born 1973
Training: Taideteollinen Korkekoulu (UIAH), Helsinki
Designs Produced By: Korhonen
Exhibitions, Honors, Other Distinctions: 2004 *Wallpaper*
    Next Generation; 2003 Palaset design competition, finalist;
    2001 Pro Finnish design, honorable mention; 2000 Finnair

Ticket Office competition (1st) (with Kai Korhonen and
    Jussi Salonen); 1997 Architecture Competition (2nd). 2003
    Established Järvi & Ruoho (with Heikki Ruoho).

JÄRVISALO, JOUKO, Finnish, born 1950
Training: Taideteollinen Korkekoulu (UIAH), Helsinki, 1977
Designs Produced By: Möbel
Exhibitions, Honors, Other Distinctions: 2002 Finndesignnow,
    Helsinki; 1999 Pro Finnish Design Prize.

JENSEN, ANNE-METTE, Danish, born 1969
Training: Det Kongelige Danske Kunstakademi, Copenhagen
Designs Produced By: Erik Jorgensen
Exhibitions, Honors, Other Distinctions: 2001 Red Dot Award,
    Germany. Practices in partnership with Morten Ernst.

JUHL, FINN, Danish, 1912–1989
Training: Det Kongelige Danske Kunstakademi (under Kaare
    Klint), Copenhagen, 1934
Designs Produced By: Hansen & Sørensen, Bovirke, France &
    Co., Bing & Grohdahl, Georg Jensen, Niels Vodder
Exhibitions, Honors, Other Distinctions: 1984 Knight,
    Order of Danneborg, Denmark; 1982 Retrospective,
    Kunstindustrimuseet, Copenhagen; 1978 Honorary Royal
    Designer for Industry, London; 1968 Two Centuries of
    Danish Design, London; 1964 A.I.D. prize, Chicago; 1954–57
    Design in Scandinavia, traveling exhibition, United States
    and Canada; 1960 Kaufmann International Design Award,
    Arts of Denmark, Metropolitan Museum, New York; 1951,
    1954, 1957 Triennale di Milano (six gold medals); 1951 Good
    Design, Chicago; 1950 Interior design of Trusteeship Council
    Chamber, United Nations Headquarters, New York, City;
    1930s fourteen prizes, Cabinetmakers' Guild exhibitions,
    Copenhagen. Works represented in major museum collec-
    tions worldwide. Also designed wood tableware.

KANDELL, JOHN, Swedish, 1925–1991
Designs Produced By: Kallemo AB
Exhibitions, Honors, Other Distinctions: 1989 Design award,
    Dagens Nyheter; Represented in many international exhi-
    bitions. Works in collections including Nationalmuseet,
    Stockholm; Röhsska Museet, Göteborg; Malmö Museum,
    Norrköping museum; Swedish Arts Council. Also designs
    glass, textiles.

KARPF, PETER, Danish, born 1940
Training: As cabinetmaker, 1957; Kunsthåndvaerkerskolen,
    Copenhagen, 1961
Designs Produced By: Iform
Exhibitions, Honors, Other Distinctions: 2002 Bruno Mathsson
    prize; 2001 Red Dot Award, Germany; 2001, 2000 I.F. Design
    Award; 2000 I.F. Ecology Design Award; 1993 Forsnäs Prize,
    Sweden; 1964–68 Design competition awards in Denmark,
    Italy, Japan, and the United States. Work in collections
    including Museum of Modern Art, New York; Museum für
    Angewandte Kunst, München, Köln; Victoria and Albert
    Museum, London; Musée des Arts Décoratifs, Montreal;
    Design Museum, London.

KASTHOLM, JORGEN, Danish, born 1931
Training: Studied in United States, apprenticeship as
    blacksmith, Copenhagen; in architecture at Skolen for
    Boligindretning, Copenhagen, 1955–58; Partnership with
    Preben Fabricius, 1962–70
Designs Produced By: Bo-ex, Fritz Hansen, Alfred Kill, Walter
    Knoll
Exhibitions, Honors, Other Distinctions: 1969 German Design
    Council award; 1968 Illums Prize; 1960s represented in
    exhibition at Musée des Arts Décoratifs, Paris, and others in
    Europe and the United States.

KJAER, JACOB, Danish, 1896–1957
Training: As cabinetmaker, 1918–20; Institute of Arts & Crafts
    Museum, Berlin
Exhibitions, Honors, Other Distinctions: 1951 Triennale
    di Milano; 1939 New York World's Fair; 1937 Exposition
    Internationale des Arts Décoratifs et Techniques dans la Vie
    Moderne, Paris; 1935 Brussels fair; 1929 Barcelona fair. Many
    international awards. 1926 Established own Copenhagen
    workshop.

KJAERHOLM, POUL, Danish, 1929–1980
Training: Kunsthåndvaerkerskolen, Copenhagen, 1952
Designs Produced By: E. Kold Christensen, Fritz Hansen, PP
    Møbler, Rud. Rasmussen
Exhibitions, Honors, Other Distinctions: 1973 I.D. Prize; 1960
    and 1957 Triennale di Milano, grand prize; 1958 Lunning
    Prize; many other recognitions. Works in major museum
    collections including Museum of Modern Art, New York;
    Victoria and Albert Museum, London.

KJARVAL, SVEINN, Icelandic, 1919–1991
Training: Kunsthåndvaerkerskolen, Copenhagen
Influential in bringing modernist aesthetics to traditional
    Icelandic furniture forms.

KLINT, KAARE, Danish, 1888–1954
Training: Studied painting; Polytechnik, Fredericksberg;
    Techniskskol, Det Kongelige Danske Kunstakademi (under
    his father P. V. Jensen Klint and Carl Petersen), Copenhagen
Designs Produced By: Fritz Hansen, Rud. Rasmussen, Le Klint
Exhibitions, Honors, Other Distinctions: 1954 C. F. Hansen
    medal; 1949 Honorary Royal Designer for Industry,
    London; 1937 Exposition Internationale des Art Décoratifs
    et Techniques dans la Vie Moderne, Paris; 1935, Grand
    Prix, Brussels Fair; 1929 Grand Prix, Barcelona Fair; 1924
    Established furniture design department at Det Kongelige
    Danske Kunstakademi, Copenhagen. Widely regarded as
    father of modern Danish furniture design, represented in
    exhibitions and major museums.

KOCH, MOGENS, Danish, 1898–1992
Training: Det Kongelige Danske Kunstakademi, Copenhagen,
    1925
Designs Produced By: Le Klint, Rud. Rasmussen
Exhibitions, Honors, Other Distinctions: 1990 Denmark's
    National Bank Anniversary Award, Danish Design Center
    Award; 1982 Danish Furniture Manufacturers Association

Award; 1964 Cabinetmakers' Guild annual prize; 1963 C.F.
    Hansen Medal; 1938 Eckersberg Medal; 1937 Exposition
    Internationale des Arts Décoratifs et Techniques dans la Vie
    Moderne, Paris; many other exhibitions and awards.

KOIVISTO, EERO, Swedish, born 1958
Training: Taideteollinen korkeakoulu (UIAH), Helsinki, 1995;
    Konstfack, Stockholm, 1994; Parsons School of Design, New
    York, 1992
Designs Produced By: Formverk, Offecct, Skandiform, Swedese
Exhibitions, Honors, Other Distinctions: 1993–2000 Excellent
    Swedish Form. Numerous awards (as CKR) for furniture,
    exhibition and interior design. 1993 Established Claesson
    Koivisto Rune (with Mårten Claesson and Ola Rune).

KORHONEN, HARRI, Finnish, born 1946
Designs Produced By: Inno, Vivero, Avarte
Exhibitions, Honors, Other Distinctions: 2003 Habitare, Best
    in Show; 2002 Finland Now; Scandinavian Design—Beyond
    the Myth traveling exhibition, SIO Interior Design Award,
    honorable mention. From 1995, Director and chief designer
    of Inno Interior.

KOSKINEN, HARRI, Finnish, born 1970
Training: Lahti Design Institute, 1989–93; Taideteollinen
    korkeakoulu (UIAH), Helsinki, 1994–98
Designs Produced By: Arabia, Asplund, Danese, Design House
    Stockholm, Hackman, Iittala, Källemo, Woodnotes, and oth-
    ers
Exhibitions, Honors, Other Distinctions: 2005 Design Plus,
    Frankfurt; 2004 Compasso d'Oro, Milan, Interior innova-
    tion award, Cologne; 2002 I.F. design award, Germany; 2001
    Red Dot award, Germany; 2000 Design Forum Finland;
    2000 Good Design, Chicago; 1999 Excellent Swedish Form.
    Many solo and international group exhibitions. Works in
    museum collections including Museum of Modern Art, New
    York; Museum of Art and Design, Helsinki; Finnish Glass
    Museum, Riihimäki; Iittala Glass Museum, Iittala; Chicago
    Atheneum; Fonds national d'art contemporain, Paris;
    Kunstgewerbemuseum, Berlin.

KOTILAINEN, ANTTI, Finnish, born 1966
Training: Lahti Design Institute
Designs Produced By: Piiroinen
Exhibitions, Honors, Other Distinctions: 2002 Good Design
    Award, Chicago.

KRAITZ, ANNA, Swedish, born 1973
Training: Academy of Fine Arts, Budapest, 1993–95; Pernbys
    Målarskol, 1995–97; Beckmans College of Design,
    Stockholm, 1997–99
Designs Produced By: Källemo
Exhibitions, Honors, Other Distinctions: 2003 IASPIS; 2002
    Ljunggrenska designer prize, Sweden.

KROGH, ERIK, Danish
Training: Journeyman joiner, 1962; Kunsthåndvaerkerskolen,
    Copenhagen, 1965
Exhibitions, Honors, Other Distinctions: 1983 Architecture

Prize; 1984 Furniture Prize, Denmark. 1975 Established own office.

KUKKAPURO, YRJÖ, Finnish, born 1933
Training: Taideteollinen Oppilaitos, Helsinki, 1954–58.
Designs Produced By: Avarte, Lepo
Exhibitions, Honors, Other Distinctions: 2003-06 Scandinavian Design Beyond the Myth traveling exhibition; 2001 Design Center Nordrhein-Westfalen; 1997 Design Nordic Way traveling exhibition; 1995 Kaj Franck Design Prize; 1991 ORNAMO Prize, Finnish Association of Designers; 1985 SIO award, Finland; 1983 Pro Finlandia medal; 1982 Artek Prize, Alvar Aalto Foundation; 1977 Illum Prize, Copenhagen; 1974 New York magazine chair competition (1st); 1966 Lunning Prize. Works in museum collections including Museum of Modern Art, New York; Victoria and Albert Museum, London; Museum of Applied Arts, Helsinki; Museum of Arts and Crafts, Hamburg; Kunstindustrimuseet, Copenhagen; Röhsska Museet, Göteborg; Nationalmuseum, Stockholm; Israel Museum, Jerusalem; Vitra Design Museum, Germany. 1959 Established Studio Kukkapuro.

LASSEN, MOGENS, Danish, 1901–1987
Training: Tekniskskol, Copenhagen, 1919–23
Designs Produced By: Rud. Rasmussen
Exhibitions, Honors, Other Distinctions: Chief architect of Den Permanente exhibitions, 1939–67. Participant in international architectural exhibitions.

LAX, ASKO, Finnish, born 1960
Training: Art Center College of Design, Pasadena, California
Designs Produced By: Piiroinen

LEINO, JOUNI, Finnish, born 1961
Training: Taideteollinen Korkekoulu (UIAH), Helsinki, 1983–90
Designs Produced By: Inno
Exhibitions, Honors, Other Distinctions: 2002 Jouni Leino Net Cafe, Stockholm; 2001 Workspheres, Museum of Modern Art, New York; 1996 I.D. Annual Design Review (honorable mention); 1987; Lahtidesign 87, Finland (1st).

LERVIK, ALEXANDER, Swedish, born 1972
Training: Carpenter apprenticeship; Beckmans School of Design, Stockholm
Designs Produced By: Skandiform
Exhibitions, Honors, Other Distinctions: 2001 Excellent Swedish Form; 2000 Premio Ambiente, Italy; 1999 Konsthantverkets prize; 1998 Young Swedish Design, Erik Berglund Prize.

LINDAU, BÖRGE, Swedish, born 1932
Training: Slöjdföreningen, Göteborg, 1957–62, (now HDK: Art School for Design and Handicraft)
Designs Produced By: Åhmans, Blå Station, Lammhults, Zero
Exhibitions, Honors, Other Distinctions: 1993 Excellent Swedish Form; 1987, 1984 Forsnäs Prize, Sweden; 1975 SID

Design award; 1969 Lunning Prize (with Bo Lindekrantz). 1964–77 Partnership Lindau & Lindekrantz (with Bo Lindekrantz). 1984 Established Blå Station.

LINDBERG, RALF, Swedish, born 1952
Training: Nykelviksskolan, 1982–83, Konstfackskolan, 1983–88 (both Stockholm)
Designs Produced By: Källemo, Gärsnäs
Exhibitions, Honors, Other Distinctions: 2001 Golden Chair award; 1998, 1995, 1992, 1991, 1989 Excellent Swedish Form; 1990, 1988 Forsnäs Prize, Sweden.

LINDEKRANTZ, BO, Swedish, born 1932
Training: Konstindustriskolan, Göteborg, 1957–62
Designs Produced By: Lammhults
Exhibitions, Honors, Other Distinctions: 1969 Lunning Prize (with Börge Lindau). 1964–77 Partnership Lindau & Lindekrantz (with Borge Lindau); from 1977 partnership with Peter Hiort-Lorentzen; 1984 Established Blå Station.

LINDFORS, STEFAN, Finnish, born 1962
Training: Taideteollinen Korkeakoulu (UIAH), Helsinki, 1988
Designs Produced By: Martela, P. O. Korhonen, Ingo Maurer
Exhibitions, Honors, Other Distinctions: 2001 Tokyo Design Award; 1996 Good Design, Chicago; 1992 Georg Jensen Prize; 1986 Triennale di Milano Medal of Honor; 2000 Solo exhibitions New York, Milan, Tokyo, and Helsinki. Permanent public sculpture installations in New York, Helsinki, other cities. Also designs lighting.

LINDVALL, JONAS, Swedish, born 1963
Training: Högskolan för Design och Konsthantverk (HDK), Göteborg, 1989–93; Guest student, Royal College of Art, London, 1992; Guest student, Det Kongelige Danske Kunstakademi, Copenhagen, 1993
Designs Produced By: David, Kockums, Skandiform
Exhibitions, Honors, Other Distinctions: 2001 Furniture design of the year, Sweden; 1998–2000 Excellent Swedish Form; 2000 Interior of the year award, Sweden (2nd); solo exhibitions in various European cities. Work in collections including Victoria and Albert Museum, London; Museum of Art, Malmö; Nationalmuseum, Stockholm.

LJUNGGREN, MATTIAS, Swedish, born 1956
Training: Konstfack, Stockholm, 1985–90
Designs Produced By: Källemo
Exhibitions, Honors, Other Distinctions: 2002 Golden Chair award, Sweden; 2001, 1998, 1991, 1989, Excellent Swedish Form, Stockholm; 1994 Nordique Profiles, Nationalmuseum, Stockholm; 1990, 1988 Forsnäs Prize, Sweden.

LÖÖF, BIRGITTA, Swedish, born 1956
Training: Högskolan för Design och Konsthantverk, 1996
Designs Produced By: Klaessons

LUDVIGSEN, PHILIP BRO, Danish, born 1962 (Australia)
Training: Kunsthåndvaerkerskolen, Copenhagen, 1989
Exhibitions, Honors, Other Distinctions: 1999 Good Design,

Chicago; 1998 Calm is a Luxury, Copenhagen; 1995 New Jungle Design, Copenhagen; 1993 New Directions in Scandinavian Design, London.

LÚTHERSSON, PETÚR B., Icelandic, born 1936
Training: Apprenticeship as cabinetmaker, Reykjavik, 1958; Kunsthåndvaerkerskolen, Copenhagen, 1961–64
Designs Produced By: Stalidjan, Labofa, Rosenthal, Tonon
Exhibitions, Honors, Other Distinctions: 2002 Pétur's Chairs, Museum of Design and Applied Art, Reykjavik; 1991 Award, Design Zentrum Nordrhein Westfalen, Essen; 1989, 1988 Designer of the Year, Iceland; 1984, 1982 Exhibition Form Island; 1982 Scandinavian Modern Design 1880–1980 traveling exhibition, United States and Canada; other international exhibitions. Also designs lighting, interiors.

MAGNUSSEN, ERIK, Danish, born 1940
Training: Kunsthåndvaerkerskolen, 1960
Designs Produced By: Engelbrechts, Fritz Hansen, Paustian, Bing & Grøndahl, Stelton
Exhibitions, Honors, Other Distinctions: 2001 Named Royal Designer for Industry, Great Britain; 1997 Design Innovations award, Germany, Good Design Gold Prize, Japan; 1996 Bindesbøll Medal; 1983 Designer of the Year, Denmark; 1977 Furniture prize, Denmark; 1967 Lunning Prize. Also designs ceramics, tableware, accessories.

MALMSTEN, CARL, Swedish, 1888–1972
Training: Pahlmanns Handelsinstitut, Kunglige Tekniska Högskolan, Stockholm; apprentice in furniture workshop with Pelle Jonsson, Stockholm, 1910–12; studied with Carl Bergstrom, Stockholm, 1912–15; Cabinetmaking and architecture apprenticeships
Designs Produced By: Carl Malmsten Möbler
Exhibitions, Honors, Other Distinctions: 1925 Exposition Internationale des Arts Décoratifs et Industriels Modernes, Paris; 1939 exhibited at New York World's Fair; 1982 Scandinavian Modern Design, 1880–1980, traveling exhibition, United States and Canada. 1916 Established freelance design practice. Classically influenced early modern designer with work in museum exhibitions worldwide.

MANNERMAA, OLLI, Finnish, 1921–1998
Designs Produced By: Martela
Exhibitions, Honors, Other Distinctions: Many awards. First Finnish designer to explore use of plastics in furniture design.

MANZ, CECILIE, Swedish, born 1972
Training: Danmarks Designskole, Copenhagen; Taideteollinen Korkeakoulu (UIAH), Helsinki, 1997
Designs Produced By: PP Møbler
Exhibitions, Honors, Other Distinctions: 2004 Danish Design Prize; Northern Lights exhibition, Tokyo; 2003 Furniture for a Famous Dane competition; E.K. Christensen award; 2002 Living in Motion, Basel.

MATHIESEN, LARS, Danish, born 1950
Training: Architecture at Det Kongelige Danske Kunstakademi, 1977
Designs Produced By: Bent Krogh, Bing & Grøndahl, Erik Jørgensen, Fora Form, Fritz Hansen, P. O. Korhonen, Rabo, Softline
Exhibitions, Honors, Other Distinctions: 1998 Danish Design Council award; 1996 Red Dot, Germany; ID Prize; 1993 Furniture Prize, Denmark; 1991 I.D. Prize, G-Mark, Japan; 1986, 1984 Excellent Swedish Form; 1984 Scan-Prize; 1980 I.D. Prize; 1978 Danish Furniture Industry's Architect Competition (1st prize). 1987–91 partner in Komplot Design (with Poul Christiansen and Boris Berlin); 1978–86, and from 1992 practice as Pelikan Design (with Niels Gammelgaard).

MATHSSON, BRUNO, Swedish, 1907–1988
Training: As cabinetmaker by his father, Karl Mathsson
Designs Produced By: Bruno Mathsson International, Fritz Hansen
Exhibitions, Honors, Other Distinctions: 1978 Royal Designer for Industry, London; 1955 Gregor Paulsson Medal, Stockholm; 1939 exhibition, Museum of Modern Art, New York; Exposition Internationale des Arts Décoratifs et Industriels Modernes, Paris; 1939 exhibited at Golden Gate Exposition, San Francisco; World's Fair, New York. Represented in international exhibitions and major museums. Practiced as Bruno Mathsson International.

MATTSON, FREDRIK, Swedish, born 1973
Training: Cabinetmaking, Stenebyskolan; Konstfack, interior and furniture design, both Stockholm; Buckinghamshire Chilterns University, exchange student, England.
Designs Produced By: Blå Station
Exhibitions, Honors, Other Distinctions: 2005 Försnas Prize, Sweden; 2004 Red Dot award, Germany, Product of the Year-Sköna Hem, Design in Sweden, London; 2003 EDIDA Award, Sweden; Golden Chair award, Sweden; Salone del Mobile, Milan; 2002 Young Swedish Design award; 1999 Röhsska Museet, Göteborg.

MOGENSEN, BØRGE. Danish, 1914–1972
Training: As cabinetmaker, 1934; Kunsthåndvaerkerskolen, 1936–38; Det Kongelige Danske Kunstakademi (under Kaare Klint), 1938–41 (both Copenhagen). Worked for Kaare Klint, Mogens Koch, others.
Designs Produced By: Fritz Hansen, Fredericia, Søborg, Karl Andersson
Exhibitions, Honors, Other Distinctions: 1972 C. F. Hansens medal; 1971 Honorary Royal Designer of Industry, London; Furniture Prize, Denmark; 1958 Cabinetmakers Guild annual prize; 1950 Eckersberg Medal; 1945 Bissens Grant. 1950 Established own office. 1940s Designed earliest modern Danish furniture for export, for Danish Cooperative Wholesale Society. Also designed textiles.

MØLLER, NIELS OTTO, Danish, 1920–1981
Training: Apprentice cabinetmaker, 1939; Designskole, Åarhus
Designs Produced By: J. L. Møller

Exhibitions, Honors, Other Distinctions: 1981, 1974 Furniture Prize, Denmark.

MORITZ, EVA, Swedish, born 1966
Training: In ceramics in Östra Grevie, metal at Nyckelviksskolan, Konstfack, Stockholm
Designs Produced By: Swedese

MORITZ, PETER, Swedish, born 1964
Training: Konstfack, Stockholm
Designs Produced By: Swedese

NISSEN, SØREN, Danish, born 1944
Training: Cabinetmaking, Rud. Rasmussen, Copenhagen, Kunsthåndvaerkerskol, 1968
Designs Produced By: Aksel Kjersgaard, Bernstorffminde, P. J. Furniture
Exhibitions, Honors, Other Distinctions: Numerous medals, awards, grants and honors. Participated in exhibitions in Europe, Japan, and United States. 1970 Established partnership with Ebbe Gehl.

NØRSGAARD, ANDERS, Danish, born 1958
Training: Århus School of Architecture, 1989
Designs Produced By: Globe

NILSEN, TORSTEIN, Norwegian, born 1951
Training: Statens Håndverks-og Kunstindustriskole (SHKS), Oslo, 1975, 1991
Designs Produced By: Vatne
Exhibitions, Honors, Other Distinctions: 1986 Good Design, Sweden. Designs in partnership with Sigurd Ström.

NORDSTROM, KAJSA, Swedish, born 1973
Training: School of Design and Crafts at Göteborg University, 1998
Designs Produced By: Klaessons

NURMESNIEMI, ANTTI, Finnish, 1927–2003
Training: Taideteollinen Oppilaitos, Helsinki, 1947–50
Designs Produced By: Artek, Cassina, Merivaara, Piiroinen, Tecta
Exhibitions, Honors, Other Distinctions: 1975 Finnish State Design Award; 1964 Triennale di Milano (with Vuokko Nurmesniemi); 1960, 1957 Triennale di Milano; 1959 Lunning Prize. 1956 Established own design studio. Work represented in museum collections and exhibitions worldwide.

OPSVIK, PETER, Norwegian, born 1939
Training: Kunsthåndtverkskole, Bergen, 1959–63; Statens Håndverks-og Kunstindustriskole (SHKS), Oslo, 1963–64
Designs Produced By: Stokke, Håg
Exhibitions, Honors, Other Distinctions: 2003 Classic prize, Norway; 1999–2002 "Movement-Peter Opsvik" traveling exhibition, Munich, London, Glasgow, Ghent; 1989 Furniture Design of Year; 1986 Jacobs Prize; 1982 in Scandinavian Modern Design 1880–1980 traveling

exhibition, United States and Canada. Also known for sculpture. 1972 Established own office.

ÓSKARSDÓTTIR, ERLA SÓLVEIG, Icelandic, born 1957
Training: Danmarks Designskole, Copenhagen
Designs Produced By: Hansen & Sørensen
Exhibitions, Honors, Other Distinctions: 1999 Best of NeoCon, Chicago, Icelandic Furniture Design Day prize; 1998 IF Product Design Award; Red Dot Award, Germany.

PAAKKANEN, MIKKO, Finnish, born 1975
Training: School of Arts and Crafts, Vihti, 1991–94; Taideteollinen Korkekoulu (UIAH), Helsinki, 1998
Designs Produced By: Avarte
Exhibitions, Honors, Other Distinctions: 2002 Two Faces One Design, Museum of Industrial Art, Helsinki; 2000 Youngs Forum 2000, Design Forum, Helsinki.

PANTON, VERNER, Danish, 1926–1998
Training: Technical School, Odense, 1944–47, Det Kongelige Danske Kunstakademi, Copenhagen, 1947–51
Designs Produced By: Fritz Hansen, Herman Miller, Louis Poulsen, PP Møbler
Exhibitions, Honors, Other Distinctions: 1992 IF Prize, Japan; 1981, 1968, 1963, A.I.D. United States; 1999 exhibiton Verner Panton–Vision & Play, Copenhagen. 1951 worked with Arne Jacobsen, 1955–61 own practice in Denmark, from 1963 in France, then Switzerland. Works in many exhibitions and museum collections worldwide. Celebrated also for innovative lighting and textile design.

PEDERSEN, THOMAS, Danish, born 1971
Training: Åarhus School of Architecture, 2002
Designs Produced By: Fredericia

PETERSEN, SOREN ULRIK, Danish, born 1961
Training: As cabinetmaker, Copenhagen, 1985; Danmarks Designskole, 1990
Designs Produced By Eilersen, Fritz Hansen, Louis Poulsen, Piiroinen, PP Møbler, Royal Copenhagen
Exhibitions, Honors, Other Distinctions: 1997 Design Nordic Way traveling exhibition; 1996 SE and DDC competitions (1st prize), Denmark; 1994 *Bo Bedre* award. Also designs tableware.

PETURSDOTTIR, KATRIN, Icelandic, born 1967
Training: École Supérieure de Design Industriel, Paris, 1989–95
Designs Produced By: Swedese
Exhibitions, Honors, Other Distinctions: Represented in many group exhibitions in Scandinavia and elsewhere. Often designs in collaboration with husband Michael Young.

PLOUG, HANS CHRISTIAN, Danish, born 1962
Training: Det Kongelige Danske Kunstakademi, School of Architecture
Designs Produced By: Karl Andersson
Designs in partnership with Michael Poulsen.

POULSEN, MICHAEL, Danish, born 1974
Training: Det Kongelige Danske Kunstakademi, School of
    Architecture
Designs in partnership with Hans Christian Ploug.

RASMUSSEN, JØRGEN, Danish, born 1931
Training: Århus School of Architecture, Denmark
Designs Produced By: Fritz Hansen, Kevi
Exhibitions, Honors, Other Distinctions: Head of Institute of
    Industrial Design, School of Architecture, Århus. Several
    awards, represented in international exhibitions. From 1957
    partner in architectural office with twin brother Ib.

RASMUSSEN, LEIF ERIK, Danish, born 1942
Training: Cabinetmaker apprentice, A. J. Iversen, 1962;
    Kunsthåndvaerkerskolen, 1968 (both Copenhagen)
Designs Produced By: Hansen & Sørensen, Paustian
Exhibitions, Honors, Other Distinctions: 1968 Danmarks
    Designskole, silver medal. 1978 Established Rasmussen &
    Rolff (with Henrik Rolff).

RELLING, INGMAR, Norwegian, 1920–2002
Training: Statens Håndverks-og Kunsthøgskole, Stockholm,
    taught by Arne E. Holm and Arne Korsmo, 1943–47
Designs Produced By: Rybo
Exhibitions, Honors, Other Distinctions: 1999 Norwegian
    Royal gold medal; 1997 Design Nordic Way, Sweden; 1992
    Classic Furniture design award; 1978 Jacobs Prize, Norway;
    1966 Norwegian Design Award; 1982 Scandinavian Modern
    Design 1880–1980, traveling exhibition, Canada and United
    States. Works in major museum collections, Oslo, London,
    New York, others.

ROLFF, HENRIK, Danish, born 1944
Training: Cabinetmaker apprentice, Hellerup, 1964;
    Kunsthåndvaerkerskolen, Copenhagen, 1968
Designs Produced By: Hansen & Sørensen, Paustian, Fritz
    Hansen, Bent Krogh
Exhibitions, Honors, Other Distinctions: 1968 Danmarks
    Designskole, bronze medal; 1967 Nursery Furniture
    Competition, United States (2nd prize). Partner in
    Rasmussen & Rolff (with Leif Erik Rasmussen) from 1978.

RUNE, OLA, Swedish, born 1963
Training: Konstfack, Stockholm, 1994, Det Kongelige Danske
    Kunstakademi, Copenhagen, 1992
Designs Produced By: David Design, Formverk, Offecct,
    Swedese
Exhibitions, Honors, Other Distinctions: Numerous awards
    (as CKR) for furniture, exhibition, and interior design. 1993
    Established Claesson Koivisto Rune (with Mårten Claesson
    and Eero Koivisto).

RUOHO, HEIKKI, Finnish, born 1969
Training: Taideteollinen Korkekoulu (UIAH), Helsinki, Lahti
    Design Institute
Designs Produced By: HKT Korhonen
Exhibitions, Honors, Other Distinctions: Awards in several

design competitions. 2003 Established Järvi & Ruoho with
Teemu Järvi.

SAARINEN, ELIEL, Finnish, 1873–1950
Training: Taideteollinen Korkeakoulu (UIAH), Helsinki, 1893
Designs Produced By: Adelta, International Silver,
    others
Exhibitions, Honors, Other Distinctions: 1937 Exposition
    Internationale des Arts Décoratifs et Techniques dans la
    Vie Moderne, Paris; 1934, 1929 Industrial Art exhibitions,
    Metropolitan Museum of Art; 1932 Detroit Institute of
    Arts; 1922 Chicago Tribune Tower design competition (2nd);
    1900 Finnish pavilion, Exposition Universelle, Paris. Work
    in collections including Metropolitan Museum of Art,
    New York; Courtauld Institute of Art, London; Cranbrook
    Art Museum, Bloomfield Hills. From 1926, as president of
    Cranbrook Academy of Art in Bloomfield Hills, Michigan,
    trained some of America's most important modern design-
    ers, including his son Eero. Also noted for architecture and
    metalwork designs.

SAARNIO, TIMO, Finnish, born 1944
Training: Taideteollinen Oppilaitos, 1971
Designs Produced By: Martela, P. O. Korhonen
Exhibitions, Honors, Other Distinctions: 1997 Three-Year
    State Artist Grant; 1996 International Furniture Design
    Competition, Japan; 1996, 1990 State Prize for Crafts and
    Design.

SALTO, KASPER, Danish, born 1967
Training: As cabinetmaker; Danmarks Designskole,
    Copenhagen, 1989–94, Art Center, Switzerland, 1993
Designs Produced By: Fritz Hansen
Exhibitions, Honors, Other Distinctions: 2005 Knud V.
    Engelhardt's; 2000 Erik Herløw's Scholarship; 1999 I.D.
    award; 1999 G-mark, Japan; 1999 National Bank Anniversary
    Foundation sward; 1997 Christian Grauballe's Memorial
    Scholarship; 1996 Forsnäs 100-year competition (2nd).

SANDELL, THOMAS, Swedish, born 1959
Training: Kungliga Tekniska Högskolan, Stockholm, 1985
Designs Produced By: Artek, Asplund, B&B Italia, Cappellini,
    CBI, Gärsnäs, Fogia, IKEA, Källemo, Mobileffe, Offecct,
    R.O.O.M., Rydéns, Swedese
Exhibitions, Honors, Other Distinctions: 1995 Salone
    Internazionale del Mobile; Milan; numerous group exhibi-
    tions and awards. 1995 Founded Sandellsandberg (with Ulf
    Sandberg and Joakim Uebel).

SCHWARZER, CHRISTINE, Danish, born 1971
Training: Danmarks Designskole, Copenhagen, Taideteollinen
    Korkekoulu (UIAH), Helsinki
Designs Produced By: Swedese

SEBTON, ANYA, Swedish, born 1966
Training: Nyckelvik Art and Design school, 1986–87,
    Beckmans School Of Design, Stockholm, 1993–96
Designs Produced By: Lammhults, Lustrum, Pukeber, Zero

Exhibitions, Honors, Other Distinctions: 1998 Designer for Bo Bedre. Work shown at several international exhibitions.

SÖDERBERG, PER, Swedish
Designs Produced By: David, IKEA
Practices as Per Söderberg Arkitektkontor, Stockholm.

SØRENSEN, JOHNNY, Danish, born 1944
Training: Carpentry at Helsingør Shipyard, 1963, Kunsthåandvaerkerskolen, Copenhagen, 1966
Designs Produced By: Erik Boisen, Fredericia, Magnus Olesen
Exhibitions, Honors, Other Distinctions: 1996 IF Award, Germany; 1992 Bruno Mathsson Award; 1989 G-Mark, Japan; 1978 Furniture Prize, Denmark; 1978 Institute of Business Designers Award, United States; 1971 Danish Furniture Manufacturers award; 1968 Cabinetmakers Guild award; 1966 Cabinetmakers Guild anniversary exhibition (1st). 1982 Scandinavian Modern Design 1890–1990, traveling exhibition, United States and Canada; 1966–94 worked in partnership with Rud Thygesen; 1994 Established own studio.

SORSA, RAUNO, Finnish
Training: Taideteollinen Korkeakoulu (UIAH), Helsinki, 1969
Designs Produced By: HKT Korhonen
Exhibitions, Honors, Other Distinctions: 1999 Profiles 69, Museum of Art and Design; 1997 Design Finlandais, Helsinki; 1994 Huonekaluja 25, Design Forum, Helsinki.

STENROS, PIRKKO, Finnish, 1928
Training: Taideteollinen Korkeakoulu (UIAH), Helsinki, 1951
Designs Produced By: Muurame
Exhibitions, Honors, Other Distinctions: 1993 Kaj Franck Prize, 1969 Finnish State Design Prize. Work represented in many exhibitions and museum collections. 1954 Founded architectural consultancy with husband, Helmer Stenros. First female furniture designer in Finland, and pioneer designer of modular storage furniture.

STEPP, TOM, Danish, born 1950
Training: Det Kongelige Danske Kunstakadem, Copenhagen
Designs Produced By: Fredericia, Stouby
Exhibitions, Honors, Other Distinctions: Several awards for lighting and furniture designs.

STRAND, CHRISTINA, Danish, born 1968
Training: Danmarks Designskole, industrial design, 1994
Designs Produced By: Fredericia, Tranekaer
Exhibitions, Honors, Other Distinctions: 2002 Danish Furniture award for Crown Prince competition. Work represented in various group exhibitions. Practices as Strand-Hvass, with Niels Hvass.

STRÖM, SIGURD, Swedish
Training: SHKS, Oslo, 1975, 1991
Designs Produced By: Vatne
Exhibitions, Honors, Other Distinctions: 1986 Good Design, Sweden. Practices in partnership with Torstein Nilsen.

STURE, ALF, Norwegian, 1915–2000
Training: Statens Handvverks-og Kunstindustriskole, Oslo, 1940; apprentice in cabinetmaking
Designs Produced By: Ellingsen, Lannem Keramikk, Tonning
Established own design studio, 1950. Also designed interiors, ceramics.

SUPPANEN, ILKKA, Finnish, born 1968
Training: Technillinen Korkeakoulu, Taideteollinen Korkeakoulu (UIAH), Helsinki; Gerrit Rietvelt Academy, Amsterdam
Designs Produced By: Cappellini, Proventus, Snowcrash
Exhibitions, Honors, Other Distinctions: 2000 Young Designer of Year, Finland; 1998 Dedalus Prize for young European designers; 2000 Young Nordic Design: The Generation X international traveling exhibition. Work included in several exhibitions worldwide, including Venice Architecture Biennale and Museum of Modern Art, New York; in permanent collections at Stedjelik Museum, Amsterdam and Museum fur Angewandte kunst, Cologne. 1995 Established Studio Ilkka Suppanen; 1996 Co-founded Snowcrash design cooperative.

SVEIAN, ROGER, Norwegian, born 1970
Training: Akerkshus University College, Norway
Designs Produced By: Leads, Mokasser
Exhibitions, Honors, Other Distinctions: 2005 Designer of the Year, Norway; 2004 Best Norwegian Design. Work in collection of craft museum, Bergen.

TAPIOVAARA, ILMARI, Finnish, 1914–1999
Training: Taideteollisuus-Keskuskoulu, Helsinki, 1937
Designs Produced By: Aero, Asko, Hackman, Heal's, Lukkiseppo
Exhibitions, Honors, Other Distinctions: 1990 Furniture design prize, SIO, Finland; 1971, Finnish State Design Prize; 1963, 1960, 1957, 1954 Triennale di Milano, gold medals; 1959 Pro Finlandia medal; 1952–53 visiting professor, Illinois Institute of Technology, Chicago; 1951 Good Design, Chicago. Designs represented in many museum collections.

THESELIUS, MATS, Swedish, born 1956
Training: Konstfackskolan, Stockholm, 1979–84
Designs Produced By: Källemo, Move Möbler
Exhibitions, Honors, Other Distinctions: 1998 Red Dot award, Germany; 1997 Bruno Mathsson prize; 1995 Excellent Swedish Form; 1993 Nordic Light, London; 1991 *Dagens Nyheter* design prize; 1984: IKEA scholarship. Work in collections including Nationalmuseum, Stockholm; Röhsska Museet, Göteborg; Malmö museum; Kunstindustrimuseum, Copenhagen; Sky City, Arlanda (Stockholm airport); Museum of Arts & Design, New York; Russian State Art Collection, Moscow.

THYGESEN, RUD, Danish, born 1932
Training: Kunsthåandvaerkerskolen, furniture design, 1966
Designs Produced By: Erik Boisen, Fredericia, Magnus Olesen, Niels Roth Andersen

Exhibitions, Honors, Other Distinctions: 1970 King's Furniture
Design for King Frederik IX, 1998 Lifelong Grant from
Danish Arts Foundation; 1996 I.F. Prize, Hanover; 1994
MMI Prize; 1992 Bruno Mathsson Award; 1978 Institute
of Business Designers Award, United States; 1975, 1969
Denmark's National Bank, Anniversary-Scholarship; 1971
Danish Furniture design Manufacturer's Prize of Honor;
1968 Carpenter Union's Anniversary Exhibition (1st prize).
1966–94 worked in partnership with Johnny Sørensen.

TORHAUG, CATHRINE, Norwegian
Designs Produced By: Torh Møbler

UTZON, JØRN, Danish, born 1918
Training: Det Kongelige Danske Kunstakademi, Copenhagen,
1942
Designs Produced By: Bahnsen Collection/Trioline
Exhibitions, Honors, Other Distinctions: 2003 Pritzker
Architecture Prize; 1957 Competition for Sydney Opera
House, Australia. Primarily known as architect, also designs
furniture and lighting.

VERDE, JOHAN, Norwegian, born 1964
Training: Statens Håndverks-og Kunstindustriskole, metal-
work 1985–87, industrial design 1987–89
Designs Produced By: Fora Form
Exhibitions, Honors, Other Distinctions: 2002, 1999, 1997, 1996
Norwegian Design Awards; 2002 Form 2002, Oslo.

VODDER, ARNE, Danish, born 1926
Training: Skolen for Boligindretning (under Finn Juhl),
Copenhagen
Designs Produced By: Bovirke, Erik Jørgensen, Fritz Hansen,
Kirkodan, Sibast
Exhibitions, Honors, Other Distinctions: Represented in many
exhibitions in Brussels, New York, Paris, Vienna, Zurich and
the Nordic countries.

VODDER, NIELS, Danish, 1892–1982
Exhibitions, Honors, Other Distinctions: Participated regularly
in Cabinetmakers' Guild Exhibitions, 1927–57, Copenhagen,
crafting furniture by Finn Juhl and Arne Jacobsen as well as
his own designs. Also produced prototypes for Trusteeship
Council Chamber in United Nations Headquarters, New
York City. Closed in 1970, the Vodder workshop has been
reestablished by his grandson.

VOLL, ESPEN, Norwegian, born 1965
Training: Kunsthøyskolen, Oslo, 1989, 1997
Designs Produced By: David Design, Globe, Habitat, Hovden,
Iform, LK Hjelle, Pure Design, Swedese, Vestre
Exhibitions, Honors, Other Distinctions: 2000–5 honored by
Norwegian Design Council; 2004 Wallpaper Interior design
award; Bruno Mathsson award; 2003 Elle Designer of the
Year; 2001, 2000 Salone Internazionale del Mobile, Milan;
Designers Block, London. Exhibitions in Brussels, New York,
Stockholm, and Tokyo. 2003 Established Norways Says (with
Torbjørn Anderssen and Andreas Engesvik).

VOLTHER, POUL M., Danish, 1923–2001
Training: As cabinetmaker, Danmarks Designskole
Designs Produced By: Erik Jørgensen
Exhibitions, Honors, Other Distinctions: Represented in exhi-
bitions of important mid-twentieth-century Danish design.

VON SCHEWEN, ANNA, Swedish, born 1965
Training: Högskolan för Design och Konsthantverk, Göteborg,
1990–92;, Konstfackskolan, Stockholm, 1995
Designs Produced By: CBI, Gärsnäs, IKEA; Pukeberg
Exhibitions, Honors, Other Distinctions: 2002, 1999, 1998
Excellent Swedish Form; 2003 Danish Design Center,
Copenhagen; 2002 Designers Block, London; Totem Gallery,
New York; 2001 Strictly Swedish, Washington, D.C. and
New York. Represented in exhibitions in Amsterdam,
Copenhagen, New York, Stockholm, Tokyo, Verona,
Washington, D.C. Works in collections including Stedelijk
Museum, Amsterdam, and Nationalmuseum, Stockholm.

VOSS, MORTEN, Danish, born 1963
Training: Self-trained after studies in art history
Designs Produced By: Fritz Hansen
Exhibitions, Honors, Other Distinctions: 1999 Carlsberg
Foundation Grant.

WANSCHER, OLE, Danish, 1903–1985
Training: Det Kongelige Danske Kunstakademi , Copenhagen,
1929
Designs Produced By: A. J. Iverson, Rud. Rasmussen, P. J.
Furniture
Exhibitions, Honors, Other Distinctions: 1966 Georg Jensen
competition; 1960 Triennale di Milano gold medal; 1958
Formes Scandinaves, Musée des Arts Décoratifs, Paris; 1937
Exposition Internationale des Arts Décoratifs et Techniques
dans la Vie Moderne, Paris. Professor for almost twenty years
at the department founded by Kaare Klint, Vodder; authored
influential books on historic furniture and interior design.

WEGNER, HANS, Danish, 1914–2007
Training: Trained as carpenter, 1931; Danish Institute of
Technology, 1936; Akademiets Arkitektskole, 1936–38 (both
Copenhagen)
Designs Produced By: Johannes Hansen, Carl Hansen, Erik
Jørgensen, Erik Møller & Flemming Lassen, Fredericia, Fritz
Hansen, Getama, Knoll, PP Møbler
Exhibitions, Honors, Other Distinctions: 1997 Honorary
Doctorate, Royal College of Art, London; 1997 International
Design Award, Japan; 1995 Member of Honor, Academy
of Wonderful Arts; Triennale di Milano 1954 gold medal,
1957 silver medal; 1951 Lunning Prize. Work in virtually
every international exhibition of mid-twentieth-century
design, and in permanent design collections of museums
worldwide.

WIHERHEIMO, YRJÖ, Finnish, born 1941
Training: Taidetiollinen Korkeakoulu (UIAH), Helsinki
Designs Produced By: Vivero, Asko, Haimi, Klaessons
Exhibitions, Honors, Other Distinctions: Multiple design
awards in Finland and abroad. Works represented in major

international exhibitions. Designs in permanent collections including Victoria and Albert Museum, London; Cooper-Hewitt Museum, New York; Kunstgewerbe Museum, Hamburg; Kunstindustrimuseet, Oslo; Museum of Applied Arts, Helsinki; Kunstindustrimuseet, Copenhagen; Athenaeum, Chicago. 1969 Established own office; from 1980 artistic director of Vivero Oy.

WIRKKALA, TAPIO, Finnish, 1915–1985
Training: Taidetiollinen Korkeakoulu (UIAH), Helsinki, 1933–36
Designs Produced By: Iittala, Hackman, Rosenthal, Venini
Exhibitions, Honors, Other Distinctions: 1980 Prince Eugen's Medal, Sweden; 1971 honorary doctorate Royal College of Arts; honorary member Worshipful Company of Goldsmiths, London; 1964 Honorary Royal Designer of Industry, London; 1951–54, 1960, 1963 Triennale di Milano multiple awards; 1958 exhibited at Brussels World Fair; 1951 Lunning Prize; *House Beautiful's* Most Beautiful Object of 1951; 1946 Iittala Glassworks design competition. Work represented in exhibitions and museum collections worldwide. Known primarily for glass and ceramic design, also worked in wood, silver, sculpture, and exhibition design.

Selected Bibliography

Aav, Marianne, and Kaj Kalin. *Suomalainen Muoto: Form Finland*. Helsinki: Taideteollisuusmuseo, 1986.

Aav, Marianne, and Nina Stritzler-Levine. *Finnish Modern Design*. New York: Bard Graduate Center/Yale University Press, 1998.

Beer, Eileene Harrison. *Scandinavian Design: Objects of a Life Style*. New York: American-Scandinavian Foundation, 1975.

Bowman, Monica, et al. *Svenska Möbler, 1890–1990*. Sweden: Signum, 1991.

Dahlbeck-Letterman, Helena, and Marianne Uggla, eds. *The Lunning Prize*. Stockholm: Nationalmuseum, 1966.

Design in Finland. Annual. Helsinki: Finnish Foreign Trade Association.

Donnelly, Marian C. *Architecture in the Scandinavian Countries*. Cambridge: MIT Press, 1992.

Dybdahl, Lars. *Dansk Design, 1910–1945*. Copenhagen: Kunstindustrimuseet, 1997.

Fiell, Charlotte J., and Peter Fiell. *Scandinavian Design*. Cologne: Taschen, 2003.

Hagstromer, Denise. *Swedish Design*. Stockholm: The Swedish Institute, 2001.

Halén, Widar, and Kerstin Wickman, eds. *Scandinavian Design Beyond the Myth: Fifty Years of Design from the Nordic Countries*. Copenhagen: Arvinius/Form Forlag, 2003.

Hansen, Per H., and Klaus Petersen. *250 Dansk Design Møbler*. Copenhagen: Aschenhoug, 2004.

Hard af Segerstad, Ulf (Nancy and Edward Maze, trans.). *Scandinavian Design*. Copenhagen: Gyldendalske Boghandel, 1961.

Hjort, Ebsbjorn (Eve M. Wendt, trans.). *Modern Danish Furniture*. New York: Architectural Book Publishing Co., 1956.

Hopstock, Carsten. *Norwegian Design: From the Viking Age to the Industrial Revolution*. Oslo: Dreyers Forlag, 1960.

Jalk, Grete, ed. *Forty Years of Danish Furniture Design: The Copenhagen Cabinet-Makers' Guild Exhibitions, 1927–1966*. Copenhagen: Teknologisk Instituts Forlag, 1987.

Lassen, Erik. *The Arts of Denmark*. Copenhagen: Danish Society of Arts & Crafts, 1960.

Lincoln, Louise, ed. *The Art of Norway, 1715–1914*. Minneapolis: Minneapolis Museum of Art, 1978.

Lutteman, Helena Dahlback, and Marianne Uggla, eds. *The Lunning Prize*. Sweden: Risbergs, 1986.

McFadden, David Revere, ed. *Scandinavian Modern Design, 1889–1980*. New York: Harry N. Abrams, 1982.

Moller, Svend Erik (Mogens Kaj-Larsen, trans.). *Danish Design*. Copenhagen: Det Danske Selskab, 1974.

Oda, Noritsugo. *Danish Chairs*. San Francisco: Chronicle, 1997.

Polster, Bern. *Design Directory Scandinavia*. San Francisco: Universe, 2001.

Reyer, Kras et al. *The Nordic Transparency*. Amsterdam: Stedelijk Museum, 1999.

Sieck, Frederik. *Contemporary Danish Furniture Design, Revised*. Copenhagen: Nyt Nordisk Forlag Arnold Busck, 1990.

Stenros, Anne, ed. *Visions of Modern Finnish Design*. Helsinki: Otava, 1999.

Sommar, Ingrid. *Scandinavian Style*. London: Carlton, 2003.

Virginia Museum of Fine Arts. *Design in Scandinavia* (exhibition catalog). Richmond, VA: Virginia Museum of Fine Arts, 1954.

Widenheim, Celia, ed. *Utopia & Reality: Modernity in Sweden, 1900–1960*. New York: Bard Graduate Center/Yale University Press, 2002.

Willcox, Donald, and Ove Hector. *Finnish Design: Facts and Fancy*. New York: Van Nostrand, 1973.

Zahle, Erik, ed. *A Treasury of Scandinavian Design*. New York: Golden Press, 1961.

Index of Producers

Index of Designers

Index of Model Names

About the CD-ROM

The accompanying CD-ROM contains printable JPEG files of all the images in the book.

With the appropriate graphics software, the CD images can be used by designers in developing concepts and preparing presentations for clients. Although the images are primarily intended for on-screen display, they can also be printed on either a black and white or color printer.

Further information about the image formats can be found on the readme.txt file on the CD.

The images in this book and on the CD-ROM are the property of the manufacturers listed in the credits, and may not be used commercially without their express permission.

Contents

Part I
Images 1-001–1-069

Part II
Dining & Occasional Chairs
Images 2-001 –2-056

Lounge Chairs
Images 2-0057–2-137

Stacking Chairs
Images 2-138–2-169

Desk Chairs
Images 2-170–2-180

Sofas, Love Seats, Chaises, & Sectionals
Images 2-181–2-262

Benches & Stools
Images 2-263–2-294

Dining Tables
Images 2-295–2-315

Coffee & Occasional Tables
Images 2-316–2-349

Storage, Shelves, & Room Dividers
Images 2-350–2-378

Miscellaneous
Images 2-379–2-404